W9-AES-851

The Technical Production Handbook

A Guide for Performing Arts Presenting Organizations and Touring Companies

By M. Kay Barrell

Published by
Western States Arts Federation (WESTAF)

Western States Arts Federation (WESTAF)
236 Montezuma Avenue
Santa Fe, NM 87501
505/988-1166
TDD available

Cover:
ODC/San Francisco
Photo: Lois Greenfield

The Paul Taylor Dance Company
Photo: Jack Mitchell

This book was originally made possible by a grant from the National
Endowment for the Arts, a federal agency.

Editor:	Mimi McKell
Editorial Assistance:	Patricia Nelson
Design:	Judy Anderson,
	Anderson & Helms Cook, Seattle, WA
Typography:	Xerox Ventura Publishing
Printing:	Publishers Press, Salt Lake City, UT

Special thanks to The Xerox Foundation for contributing the Xerox
Ventura Publisher Software used to produce this publication.
This 1991 edition is made possible in part by the generous
support and assistance of Publishers Press.

Library of Congress Cataloging-in-Publication Data
Barrell, M. Kay, 1945-
     The technical production handbook / by M. Kay Barrell
          p.   cm.
     ISBN 0-9611710-6-5
     1. Performing arts--Production and direction--Handbooks, manuals,
     etc. 2. Dance production--Handbooks, manuals etc.   I. Title
     PN1590.P74B37 1991
     792' .023--dc20   90-50991
                                      CIP

ISBN 0-9611710-6-5

Publisher's Acknowledgements
WESTAF extends its sincere gratitude to Mimi McKell, Director of
Performing Arts from 1986 to 1991, for her thorough and capable work
in managing and editing the revised edition of this technical assistance
aid for presenters of performing arts. Ms McKell's expertise in this area
is outstanding and was invaluable in her coordination of WESTAF's
performing arts programs.
Editor's Acknowledgements
Special thanks goes to three people with extensive experience in the
presentation and production of dance and theater who read and
commented on the manuscript: Fred Allen, Ian Rosenkranz,
and especially Phill Lipman -- who provided advice and encouragement
from beginning to end.
Mimi McKell

Contents

Introduction

This handbook is designed for specific use by performing arts presenters and touring companies. These performing companies -- theater, opera, ballet, modern dance, and an infinite number of variations on them -- offer an audience a great variety of style, scale, and quality. At the same time, these companies pose an immense range of production requirements, challenges, and occasionally headaches to a presenter.

Knowing how to select the proper production for a facility helps both the presenter and the performers to succeed and avoid many of the technical headaches that can make performing and presenting a less than pleasant experience. A basic knowledge of the technical aspects of production will help a presenter understand the needs of touring companies as well as the capabilities and limitations of the theatre space and its equipment. Thus, this handbook stresses the **basics** of technical production. Its purpose is not to turn a presenter into a lighting designer or technical director, but to allow that presenter to make more intelligent choices in the companies selected to perform and in the ways the operation of the organization is handled.

This book is written with an emphasis on presenting dance. The reason for this is that there is more dance on tour in the United States than any of the other performing arts, with the exception of classical music which doesn't have heavy technical production demands. Although the number of touring dance companies has declined since the heyday of the mid-seventies, their number is still far greater than the number of touring theater and opera groups.

Dance has more inherent pitfalls in its production requirements than does theater due to the fact that most theatres are built with the production of plays as their basic design criteria. What is appropriate for theater is not necessarily appropriate for dance. Many personnel in both managerial and technical positions come from university backgrounds where the bulk of the production is theater. Many times these people find themselves as presenters or technical directors of performing arts series with little or no experience with the quirks of presenting dance.

The first major section of this handbook deals with needs and responsibilities common to both theater and dance. The second section singles out separate production aspects of each. The third section is a glossary of terms to help the presenter understand the maze of technical language. While many of the comments are addressed directly to presenters, they also provide useful information for companies. It is hoped that this publication will help the presenter in making his or her job more pleasant, and the resulting productions more effective and successful.

Presenters
and Performers

As a presenter you have the right to expect the best possible performance from the company you have contracted. This, of course, is the common goal of both the presenter and the performer. If the best possible performance can be achieved with the least amount of frustration, headache, and extra expense, it is then more rewarding to all parties, both financially and emotionally.

The range of services and equipment required of a presenter and the theatre vary with each theatre and each engagement. Generally, the presenter will provide the theatre as well as the staff and equipment to operate the theatre properly. The better the facility, the staff, and the equipment, the easier the presenter's basic work load will be. Conversely, it is the company's obligation to give the best possible performance. To achieve this "best possible performance," it is the performers' right to expect the facilities, staff, and equipment that they were promised. The quality of the contract and the associated riders thus become a critical element in the whole booking process. Both parties must know, in a binding contractual form, what each party needs, provides, and expects of the other.

Therefore, the first critical obligation for both parties is to be very explicit and very accurate in their communications with one another, both in the contracts and verbal commitments. The performers must know exactly what they need and clearly communicate their needs to the presenter in a timely fashion. The presenter must be able to fulfill those needs or work out an agreeable compromise with the company in writing, and then be able to deliver all that has been agreed to. However, there are many scenarios that can't be written into a contract. Unforeseen things -- equipment problems, misunderstandings in communication, time overruns -- all need to be dealt with. The better organized and informed both parties are, the fewer unforeseen problems will occur.

There are four basic ways used by companies and presenters to communicate technical information: two are generated by the company and two are generated by the presenter. Each method of gathering information listed below has its merits, depending on the size and complexity of the performance and the needs of both parties.

Company Technical Rider

A touring company must send a sheet of specific requirements detailing their technical needs (a technical requirement or tech sheet) to the presenter as a rider or attachment to the contract. The presenter reads the requirements and either agrees to them or reaches a compromise with the company. The presenter then signs the contract and the tech rider. After the contract is signed, the presenter is bound to supply the agreed-upon items. If the presenter does not have the items agreed upon, he or she is required to obtain them somehow -- either by renting, borrowing, or purchasing them.

Company Technical Questionnaire

The company may ask the presenter to fill out a technical questionnaire and provide detailed information on the performance facility. A company technical questionnaire is not always part of the contract or rider but will often accompany them. The company's technical director or designer can then use the information to analyze the presenter's space and the available equipment, and adapt the company's requirements accordingly. He or she may still ask the presenter to supply additional equipment, but will be able to be more accurate and complete in the request. Company technical questionnaires vary greatly in their scope and complexity, but if a company asks a question, it expects -- and deserves -- a reply. It is the presenter's duty (or the chief technician's) to fill out the questionnaire completely and return it to the company as soon as possible. This is a time-consuming method of gathering information, but for those companies that need more detailed information, it is necessary, especially if the presenter does not have a technical information packet.

Presenter Technical Information Packet

A third method of information exchange is one used often by larger companies that travel in a more self-contained, fully self-equipped mode. In this situation a company asks for a technical information packet from the presenter (or the presenter can include it when returning the contract) and then uses the information to create its own technical adaption for the performance. However, a presenter's technical information packet is an invaluable tool in working with all sizes and types of touring companies. Even if an excellent technical packet takes a week of a presenter's technical director's time to generate, it is time very well spent. It is critical that this technical information is **current** and **correct**. The technical packet should be updated at least yearly; disseminating bad information is worse than disseminating no information at all.

The more detailed the information in the packet can be, the more useful it is. A Presenter Technical Information Packet **should** contain:
- A contact sheet with all the phone numbers of appropriate staff (including

technicians) and all addresses for mailing information. Include union information with Business Agent contacts if applicable.

- A general description of the facility including stage, auditorium, and support facilities.
- A detailed description of the stage with all possible dimensions.
- A detailed description of the floor including resiliency, surface, condition, whether or not it can be screwed into, etc.
- Maps for the company including directions to the facility and hotel, parking and loading information.
- A listing of theatre policies and procedures including local laws regarding smoke alarms and pyrotechnics.
- A seating chart of the theatre.
- A detailed plan of the stage.
- A detailed hanger log.
- A detailed description of the sound system including an inventory of equipment (don't forget intercom and paging systems).
- A detailed description of the lighting system including descriptions of any problems with the system. Don't forget the company switch or other hook-ups for a road board, and their location and distance from the stage.
- An accurate and detailed inventory of lighting instruments including any information about any instruments that are permanently hung such as beam slots/Front of House (F.O.H).
- A description of the F.O.H. mounting positions with distances and recommendations of best positions for different needs.
- A description of the rigging system as to type and any problems such as bent pipes, non-working line sets, permanently rigged pipes, or double purchase line sets.
- A detailed inventory of all available soft goods such as legs, borders, scrims, cycs, sky drops, travelers. Include color, dimensions, material, percentage of fullness (important information), and condition. Also mention whether the act curtain travels or draws.
- A detailed description of all dressing rooms including size, location in relation to stage and accommodations (i.e., number of people, tables, chairs, mirrors, toilets, sinks, showers). Also address laundry and wardrobe facilities.
- A description of the loading facilities including directions for the drivers, number and size of trucks that can be accommodated, height of the dock, distance to the stage, and dimensions of the smallest door between the dock and the stage.

The packet **may** contain:
- Listings of nearby hotels, restaurants (especially those open late at night), doctors, grocery stores, radio/TV stations, bars, bowling alleys and more!
- A detailed section view of the stage (especially important for large theatres).
- A listing of onstage dimmable circuits and a diagram of sound system outlets.

One-Page Facility/Technical Information Sheet

A one-page description of the facility and basic technical capabilities is a common tool for use with booking agents and company managers during the booking process. This is a valuable document and can save a lot of wasted time in determining the suitability of facilities for companies -- if it is correct. It should list the basic elements of the building including dimensions of the stage, fly loft, and auditorium, and rough descriptions of rigging, dimmer, and sound systems. It should contain basic inventories of lighting equipment and drapes. It should also address any major oddities or deficiencies unique to the facility or out of the industry norm. This one-page description should never be used as the final information source except for performers with very simple technical needs.

COMMUNICATION

The communication process between company and presenter requires the active participation of both parties and invariably involves large amounts of paperwork. If the company doesn't ask for information about your stage and equipment, but only sends a list of requirements, it often indicates potential problems or, at least, a lack of interest on the part of the company. In a situation like this it is very wise for the presenter to volunteer the technical information as well as a description of any variations between the company's list of requirements and the reality of the facility.

Every theatre ever built has its own idiosyncrasies. If there is anything strange, substandard, or extraordinary about your space or equipment, the visiting company cannot possibly know about it without being told. If you don't surprise the company with space and equipment problems, the company won't be as likely to surprise you with cost over-runs or a less than professional show.

A theatre should always be well-maintained. It should be clean. The dimmers should work. The sound system should work and work well. The draperies should be in good repair. All lighting instruments should be checked and operable. All elements of the theatre necessary to running a show should always be in good condition before any company arrives. But, if you know that something isn't going to be operating correctly, let the company know in advance. They may be able to adapt with adequate warning.

Once you, as a presenter, have agreed to furnish certain equipment, you must supply it. If you have made verbal or contractual agreements, don't forget to relay the information on to your own technical director, who is the one who ultimately bears the responsibility of making the show work. Horror stories abound about companies arriving at a theatre expecting non-existent facilities, crews, or equipment that were agreed to contractually in a technical rider by a presenter who had never read the rider or passed it on to the technical staff.

After the initial exchanges of information on paper, the best possible way to communicate is for your technical director to get on the phone far in advance of the engagement and talk directly with the person most involved in technical elements of production. This is usually the company's technical director or production manager. Presenters frequently only deal with artist management prior to the engagement. If this is the case, presenters should demand direct contact with the company at least one month prior to the engagement for a simple show and up to six months for a complex production. Remember that companies are often on the road, and establishing contact with a technical director may take several weeks.

The more directly the two technicians talk, the fewer chances there are for lapses in communication. Go over all elements of the engagement. Double check crew times and numbers. Make sure the company has received all of your technical information and that it's not sitting on the agent's desk. Remind the company technician about any oddities or deficiencies of your space and equipment. Double check what you are to supply and what the company is to supply. Often a company will send a light plot and/or a hanger log ahead and will request that you set up the lighting in advance. Discuss any questions involving this early set-up (called pre-rigging or pre-hanging) in detail so that the lighting doesn't have to be hung twice. Pre-rigging or pre-hanging can be a very cost-effective measure in many instances, but only if it needs to be done once.

The dance and theater companies that tour the country today differ immensely in the size of their productions and the amount of equipment they carry. Some companies carry with them everything they could possibly need, while others have enormous productions and cannot travel with all of their own equipment; many have no equipment. The point is, don't try to second-guess the needs of any touring company. Tell them what you have so they won't be surprised, and make sure that you know their needs so that you won't be surprised. Concise, correct, and clear communication between the two parties is the single most critical element in the production business.

THE SPACE

Stage Area

A presenter will usually have access to at least one of three basic types of theatre spaces in which to present a touring company: proscenium, thrust, or arena theatres. Touring productions are usually directed and designed to fit one particular type of stage and most cannot be adapted at the last moment. Some cannot be adapted at all. Settings for a proscenium production usually will not work on a thrust stage, and a play directed for a thrust stage will probably be ineffective when pushed behind a proscenium.

Since most theatres in this country are of the proscenium type, most touring companies are geared to proscenium presentations. This is especially true of dance companies. The shapes and patterns of dance movement are usually designed to be seen from one direction only. Because entrances and exits are so important, and also because the dancers need to be hidden when they're off stage, a proscenium stage is usually required for most dance performances. For this reason most dance companies will attempt to modify thrust or arena theatres to a proscenium format. These adaptations can lead to horrible sightlines and unsalable seats.

In addition to the various types of theatre spaces, there are variations on the types of rigging systems found in these spaces. A proscenium theatre traditionally has a rigging system or fly system that allows scenery and lights to fly in and out. Arena stages are traditionally dead-hung, meaning that the pipes or gridwork above the stage area is permanently attached to the roof structure and does not move. This requires that all scenery, drapery or lighting equipment be carried up a ladder to the pipe or batten in order to be attached. With a fly or rigging system the batten is brought to the floor to attach the elements and is then "flown" out. Thrust stages often have a combination of fly system over the upstage portion of the stage and dead-hung pipes over the thrust. Since the proscenium stage traditionally has a fly system, many productions designed for a proscenium stage are designed with a fly system as an integral part of the production.

However, fly lofts are expensive to build. Due to cost and aesthetic considerations (some architects don't like to see the fly loft), many theatres -- especially in the 1950's and 1960's -- were built as proscenium theatres but without a fly loft or fly system. These dead-hung proscenium theatres are often found on college campuses. A theatre with a dead-hung stage is severely limited as to what it can produce, and requires more crew time -- and expense -- to prepare for performances. It cannot generally produce productions requiring flown scenery. There are productions that can be modified, though that depends entirely on the specific production and the inventiveness of the theatre's and company's technicians.

There is a more recent trend to building theatres that have a small fly system without a fly loft. This type of theatre cannot fly scenery out of sight in a traditional manner, but it can bring the battens down onto the stage for the attachment of scenery and lights. This type of compromise theatre is faster and therefore cheaper to rig, and much more flexible in the range of productions it can produce.

The type of performance space has a direct bearing on the type of production that will be most effective. For this reason you should let the companies that you are considering booking know exactly the type of space available before you contract with them. If you have a proscenium stage, book proscenium productions. If you have a thrust stage, book companies that are geared for thrust productions or those that are flexible enough to adapt. If you have a gymnasium, make sure either you or the company you're booking has the time and equipment to transform it into a usable performance space.

A gymnasium with its large expanse can be a very exciting space for dance if the space can be modified and if the dancers are emphasized by masking and lighting. Theater has a greater problem in a gymnasium because the acoustics of such a large hollow space are usually deadly. Hearing anyone speak in a gymnasium is a problem. It is better to arrange an arena theatre production in a more intimate space with better acoustics.

Whatever the type of space selected for the production, there are some universal considerations. The space must be clean, well-heated, and emptied of all items not to be used for this particular production. This includes band instruments in the corners, stored flats, and old drops. It is a great burden for a company with a very tight set-up schedule to have to sweep the stage, remove the tubas, and take down last year's Camelot drops before they can begin to rig their own production. Cleaning and clearing the space is not only a common courtesy, but will save you money in overtime crew costs and ragged tempers. When you tell a company that you have 40 feet of depth on the stage, they will come expecting that 40 feet. If eight feet is dedicated to an orchestra shell that cannot move anywhere else, or to last term's musical set, then you, the presenter, have created a problematic situation. The company should have been told that they had 32 feet of stage. That missing eight feet could be fatal to the production.

The space should have all needed maintenance performed on it well before the company arrives. Burned-out lamps and torn drapes will have to be remedied eventually, so it is much better to have them repaired before the tempers flair and the contracts begin waving. If the company has requested an A-frame ladder for focusing lighting instruments and yours is in storage five miles across town or a hundred yards across campus, get it before they arrive. When the company loses its set-up crew in the middle of a hectic day to look for promised equipment or to run your errands, the schedule for the entire day and possibly the performance is in jeopardy.

Dressing Rooms

Most touring performers spend more time in their dressing rooms than they do in their hotel rooms. For this reason stringent dressing room specifications are listed in most company contracts. Most dressing room clauses read something like this: "The company requires clean, well-heated, non-public dressing rooms with adequate and convenient toilet facilities, hot and cold running water, with a dressing table, a chair and a lighted mirror for each performer." AGMA and Equity union contracts will often allow a performer to refuse to perform if the dressing room requirements are not met. The temperature in a dressing room, as well as on stage, is always critical. Many contracts -- union and non-union -- will not allow a performer to perform if the temperature drops below a minimum of 68 degrees or exceeds a maximum of 92 degrees. It is therefore possible that a dancer can legally refuse to perform even though the artistic director and the presenter think everything is just fine. The presenter should be aware of the importance of adequate dressing facilities and do everything possible to accommodate these requests, not only because they are in the contract, but, more importantly, because they contribute to the comfort and state of mind of the performers.

Gymnasium performances pose special dressing room problems, depending on how the stage area is set up. Keep in mind when setting up a gymnasium space that the performers must have constant and quick access to dressing rooms for costume changes and rest periods. Gym locker rooms are at least large and can usually be modified to suit company requirements. Just make sure the performers are the only people using them. Football teams and dance companies don't mix.

"Cosmic" Space Considerations

One of the most common maladies to befall a presenter is the "quart in a pint pot" syndrome. A presenter always wants the most production possible for the dollar. The presenter's audience has always wished to have "Phantom of the Opera," "Siegfried," and "Sleeping Beauty" done in mixed rep. But it just doesn't work. Due to audience pressure, presenters continually call for larger productions than their stage can possibly accommodate. Companies continually accept engagements of their largest productions in undersized houses due to the economic pressures of booking. The ultimate losers are the audience, the presenter, and the performer. Companies have a range of repertoire. Talk to the company and select the proper performance for your particular space and audience. Don't attempt to produce pieces larger than your theatre, your staff, or your budget can accommodate.

CREWS AND TECHNICIANS

Touring companies vary greatly in the number of technicians they travel with and the size of crews they require the presenter to furnish. Any company that does a produced show will travel with some technical staff. This staff will vary in size from a single, all-purpose technician who will supervise the set-up, design the lights, and then call the cues, to a company that travels with specialists in every area.

Some companies require two or three house technicians, while larger companies may require twenty-five to thirty union stage hands. When a company makes a crew call, their own staff are not included in the numbers.

The titles used for stage technicians and crews are often deceiving and down-right confusing to the uninitiated. Some stage crew terms (i.e., prop man, flyman) are standard terms throughout the industry, but that doesn't mean that the crews in these areas have to be men. Here are some simple definitions:

- **Department head:** A stage crew is broken up into different areas of specialization. Each of these areas is called a department, and the main person in each department is the department head. Some companies adhere to this division of areas very strongly, especially yellow card companies. Other companies are very flexible in their requirements of who does what.
- **Carpenter:** A stage carpenter is one who handles the scenic elements of a production including drops and draperies, flats, wagons, and sometimes large furniture pieces. An assistant carpenter is sometimes called a grip.
- **Flyman:** The person who operates the fly or rigging system. Sometimes the flymen are their own department, and sometimes they are considered part of the carpenter crew.
- **Prop man:** A prop is any non-scenic item used on the stage such as furniture, set dressing, or any non-costumed, hand-carried item. The person that cares for these items is called the prop man. This is the catch-all position on the stage crew. The prop man is in charge of the cleanliness of the stage. He or she sets up the orchestra pit and, with dance companies, is in charge of the portable dance floor. The prop man also tends the performers with water, Kleenex, ice packs, etc.
- **Electrician:** The person who deals with anything electrical on the stage. This consists mainly of the stage lighting and dimming system but may also include chandeliers, fog machines, pyrotechnics, or any other electrified items. The follow spot operators are considered electricians.
- **Sound man:** The person in charge of the sound including the auditorium reinforcement, on-stage monitors, and the paging and intercom systems. The sound man may be his or her own department or may be considered part of the electrical crew.
- **Wardrobe:** The wardrobe department is in charge of caring for the costumes and dressing the performers. An assistant in this department is usually called a dresser.
- **Stage manager:** The person that runs the performance. He or she is the backstage boss once the performance has begun and has the responsibility of maintaining the integrity of the production. The stage manager calls all the cues for the lighting, fly system, sound, and scenic moves. With some art forms -- and especially in opera -- the stage manager tells the performers when to make entrances.
- **Running crew:** The crew that is required for the operation of the performance is called the run of show or running crew (a series of performances are called a run).
- **Load-in crew:** The crew required for the moving of the production from the trucks and setting it up prior to performance is called the load-in crew. This crew is generally larger than the run of show crew. The load-in crew may be needed for a short period of time or may be needed for a couple of days, depending on the size

of the production. (Remember that union crews have to be paid for a minimum call of four hours.) In union situations it is usually possible (depending on local rules) for a portion of the crew members to be cut or released from a crew call after the minimum four hours. This means that a number of crew members listed on the load-in crew schedule will not have to be sitting around with nothing to do.

■ **Load-out crew:** The dismantling of a production is called a strike or load-out. The load-out crew required is usually the same crew as was required for the load-in.

Union Crews

Crew types and qualities also vary greatly. A union stagehand will be a member of the I.A.T.S.E. (International Alliance of Theatrical Stage Employees). Most large civic theatres and some large university theaters require full union crews for all productions. Some large modern dance companies, most large ballet companies, and most large theater companies also require union crews. These are called yellow card companies.

A company that has signed a formal contract with the I.A.T.S.E. is required to notify and use union crews wherever there is an active I.A.T.S.E. local in the area of the theatre. The term **"yellow card"** comes literally from a yellow card that the company is required to send to the I.A.T.S.E. local notifying them that the show is coming, what the dates are, and how many crew will be required. This is the union's way of guaranteeing that the proper number and type of stagehands are called for each production. This procedure irritates some presenters because it leaves them out of the process of calling the stagehands that they are going to have to pay for. There are occasionally exceptions to this rule, and you may be able to negotiate a yellow card depending on your local conditions.

Union wages may not differ significantly from non-union wages, but the working rules may. Prior to signing the contract, the presenter should have a clear understanding of union requirements. The local business agent is obligated to explain the contents of the standard union agreement and to give a copy of it to the presenter. The smartest thing a presenter can do is to get to know the local I.A.T.S.E. business agent and develop an amicable working relationship with the union. Most university theatres have working relationships with the union local where a yellow card crew call is split between the union local members and the resident student crew. In many instances this is the most effective way to fill a crew call and it benefits everyone. The union members get to work in their chosen field (which isn't that common in many cities), and the student crews get to work with professionals and learn from them.

Union crews frighten many presenters and companies. Whether you have reason to be frightened or not depends on the organization of both the company and the presenter, and on the particular union local. Many union crews are fabulous, some are less than fabulous. The quality of the union locals vary from city to city. The keys to a good working relationship with a union crew are generally preparation and organization. The rules of the union are designed to protect the rights of the stagehands. If you know the rules and time restrictions and work within them, a union crew can be efficient and not outrageously expensive. In fact, in many circumstances it is by far the preferred type of crew. It is the meal penalties and the overtime penalties caused by poor organization that can cause trouble for a presenter. To find out the union rules and wage scales for your particular theatre, call the business agent for the union local in your area. To find the number of the union local in your area, contact the international I.A.T.S.E. office at 1515 Broadway, Suite 601, New York, NY 10036 (800-223-6872).

Non-union Crews

A company that doesn't carry a yellow card will sometimes prefer non-union crews, although every company wants the best crew available. The item most remembered by a touring technician is the quality of crews encountered. Most theatres that book a large number of engagements will have at least one full-time technical director. This technical director, who may or may not be union, is extremely important in ensuring not only that the stage runs smoothly but also that hundreds of thousands of dollars of specialized theatre equipment is handled correctly. Under this technical director there can be many different crew structures. Some theatres will use a partial union crew (or mixed crew), some will use a permanent, paid non-union crew, and some will use a full student crew, sometimes paid and sometimes not.

Student Crews

Many companies will accept a student crew. In fact, because of their energy and enthusiasm, some student crews are among the very best. There are some "musts" for a student crew, however. There must be a crew chief who stays with the company the entire time it is on stage. He or she must know where everything is stored and must have keys to every room in the theatre, as well as the authority to make decisions and control the crew. Without these capabilities a student crew chief and, therefore, the entire crew, is useless. Another "must" is that the crew members must not change from the time load-in begins until load-out is over. If the crews are constantly changing from hour to hour, there is no way a set-up can flow properly. If lighting cues are taught to one crew member and another person shows up to run the show, all the time spent with the first crew member was wasted. Training is an invaluable tool for student crews. Invest in a top-notch technical director to train and motivate the students.

Crew Calls

When a company specifies a certain number of crew members for a specific amount of time, it assumes that the set-up will be smooth and uninterrupted in an adequate space with a qualified crew. If your situation is not normal due to unusual facilities, crews, or time restrictions, let the company know this in advance and work out realistic crew calls with them. To restate the importance of communication, the best way to get problems ironed out in advance is to have your technical director talk directly with the technical director of the company. The technicians know the exact requirements of the show and the exact problems of the theatre. They'll also have more confidence in one another having aired problems or concerns before that first fateful meeting backstage.

TIME

The hanging, focusing, and setting the levels of a complex light plot takes a minimum of six hours with experienced and organized technicians. A dance company, especially ballet, or a theater company with large sets may require another full day for set-up. Wherever economically feasible a two day set-up for a large production is easier on all concerned and allows more time to solve unforeseen problems. A very large or very poorly organized production may take several days.

Most touring companies are able to estimate their time and crew requirements very accurately. Being able to stick to a set-up schedule no matter what the complications is a point of pride with many technicians. There are some companies, however, that under-estimate their set-up time even though they've been on the road for years. If available theatre time allows for miscalculations or disasters, there is much less pressure on both the theatre's crew and company's technicians. If the time schedule in the theatre is very tight and someone is scheduled to move in as soon as you're scheduled to finish, or if the facility is used for other purposes -- such as classes -- during the day, be sure to let the company know well in advance.

Another way to lessen pressure on set-up day -- and save time and money -- is to pre-rig or pre-hang all items of yours that the company plans to use such as masking, backdrops, and lighting instruments. Many companies will contractually insist that their rigging and lighting be pre-hung. This requires getting a detailed light plot and/or hanger log from the company designer in advance. The company is usually eager to do this. This can only be achieved, however, if the technical information sent to the designer by you is very detailed and accurate.

Be sure to double-check the theatre's schedule. All too often conflicts arise from double-scheduling or complete lack of scheduling in the theatre. When the swing band arrives to rehearse in the middle of the company's set-up, valuable time can be lost and tempers can flare.

EQUIPMENT

Very few companies tour with all necessary equipment. Many theater companies, and most modern dance companies, carry practically nothing but costumes and prepared scenic elements. Problems arise when the company takes facilities or equipment for granted. Unless told otherwise, the company's lighting designer or technical director will assume basic things about a theatre such as adequate masking, front-of-house mounting positions, and adequate cable to connect existing instruments to existing circuits. Assumptions like these can cause massive problems if they are incorrect. If you have a good theatre that is well-equipped and well-maintained, then these assumptions are probably valid. It is always safest, however, to check all elements of the production just to be sure.

Below is a listing of the most common items normally needed for a production that you may or may not have to furnish. Check the glossary in Chapter 3 if you are unsure of terms used.

Lighting Equipment

■ **Lighting instruments**: Lighting fixtures are referred to as instruments and typically include Lekos, Fresnels, and floodlights. Be sure to check on their condition, that all are lamped, and are of the specified wattage. On Lekos (ellipsoidal reflector spotlights), know the focal lengths of the lenses and communicate this accurately to the company. A 6 x 12 Leko cannot substitute for a 6 x 9 Leko. Focal lengths are crucial! Telling a company that you have 48 six inch Lekos is useless without the knowledge of the focal length. Refer to the glossary for more detailed explanations of the various types.

■ **Lamps**: Lamps (bulbs) for each type of instrument are very specific and are not inter-changeable. Hire a competent technician to make sure you order and use proper lamps in the proper instruments. Modern Tungsten-Halogen lamps that replace the older incandescents are very intolerant of rough handling. A $30 lamp designed to last 2000 hours will only last minutes if improperly handled.

■ **Alignment**: Alignment of the optical elements of an instrument is critical, since poor alignment can reduce the efficiency of an instrument by at least 50%. Each instrument should be checked by your technicians at least yearly to see if the output appears to be normal. While checking the alignment, make sure the lenses are clean.

■ **Dimmers**: Confirm the number of dimmers and the capacity of each. Then check to see how many are actually operating properly. The type of dimmer and its operational effectiveness are critical items to most companies. It took twenty years of transition, but computerized dimmer control boards are finally the standard of the industry. Make sure yours works properly. Being able to tell someone that you have a computer-controlled dimming system is a sham if the computer does not function properly. Since there is so little standardization of systems, the responsibility of programming and operating your dimmer board is yours. Make sure you have a pool of qualified board operators available for every production. It's your equipment and it's very expensive.

■ **Cable and connectors**: Cable is often overlooked. A theatre that uses permanently installed circuits will often own very little spare cable. A dance company that lights primarily from booms (also called trees and towers) in the wings can require enormous amounts of cable. Check the types of connectors (plugs) on all cable and instruments. There are many different types of connectors for stage use, but practically none of them are compatible. A two-prong 20 amp. twistlock, for instance, is not compatible with a three-prong grounded 20 amp. twistlock. If a company is planning to plug its instruments into your circuits (or conversely, plug your instruments into their circuits), the connectors must be compatible or someone must have adapters made with the appropriate male and female connectors. Check all cables for compatibility with equipment whether it is rented, borrowed, or provided by the company.

Color Media

Color media, often called **gels**, are plastic-based filters used to change the color of stage lamps. Gels are sometimes supplied by the presenter and sometimes by the company. Availability of specific colors can be a problem in the largest of cities and impossible in many medium and small cities. Modern dance companies compound this problem because they consistently use color that is unnatural and saturated and, therefore, often harder to find. Even a theatre with a very large stock of color media will rarely have the exact color needed for a modern dance production. Many dealers of color media won't ordinarily stock the range of color needed for a dance concert. Current practice now dictates that a company with very specific color needs should travel with its own color media. If a company doesn't carry its own color, it can't be too fussy about alternate color choices.

Masking

Dance puts much more emphasis on the quality of the masking because this is often the only setting employed. Because of this, the condition and color of the masking becomes critical for a dance concert. Dark to black is the best color. Flat sky drops are definitely better for dance backings than wrap-around cycloramas because the cycloramas hamper quick exits, entrances, and side lighting positions. Any exotic backings should be supplied by the company and not be the concern of the presenter.

Sound System

High quality music reproduction is vital for dance. High quality speech amplification is often crucial for theater. If a dance company is using its tape on your tape decks, check for compatibility with the number of tracks and whether stereo equipment is required. Many good theatres still operate single channel monaural sound systems. A theater company may expect to patch their microphones into your sound system. Again, check the system for compatibility of connectors.

Quality of sound is a very subjective point. A sound system that is considered acceptable by the theatre management may not be considered acceptable by the touring company. It is generally wise to know where you can get an alternate sound system on short notice before the company arrives. The only real guarantee a company has of good sound is if they travel with their own system.

If you, as a presenter, have to rent a sound system, go to the most reputable rental source possible. Often people who supply sound systems for rock and roll bands will be able to supply very good sound systems as bands are usually very fussy. Do remind them, however, that the system needed for a dance company is much less extensive than for rock and roll. Home systems are not appropriate for use in a theatre. If your sound system is questionable, contact the company immediately. Unlike color media, trooping an entire sound system may be completely out of the question for many companies that still require high quality sound. Couple this factor along with the subjectivity of just what constitutes good sound, and the simple issue of "sound" becomes a Pandora's Box for many presenters. Sound is another area where the quality of the technician operating the system is critical.

Rentals

After you have received the requirements of the company, and your technician has discussed the possible alternatives with the company's technical director, you must go about procuring the items that you don't have and they can't furnish. When faced with equipment rental, many presenters first think of contacting a large theatrical rental house. There are some very competent rental firms, but they are few and far between. Rental equipment can be in terrible repair and is sometimes delivered late. If the rental firm is a long distance away and the equipment arrives damaged or lacking a vital part, it will be unusable. And there might not be time to replace it.

Often the best place to rent or borrow equipment is from another theatre at a high school or university in your own town or in the next town. Renting equipment from another theatre in your area can build cooperation between groups, and the reciprocity can be beneficial for everyone. You can also save on the transportation charges.

If no equipment is available locally, and you're planning to present performing groups regularly, you should consider purchasing equipment. With the high costs of renting you could probably pay the purchase price of needed equipment within a few years. Also, if you own the equipment, you can help pay for its purchase by renting it out to other presenters or theatres when it isn't being used by you.

If you run into an absolute impasse in procuring equipment (there are times when even the largest rental firms will be unable to supply the needed items), contact the company again and explain the situation. Sometimes a change to a simpler program with simpler technical requirements is possible. If a change in program is not possible, the company will occasionally consent to perform in an under-produced situation. The presenter must be aware that such compromises can make the concert less effective than it might have been. The alternative to such a compromise is cancellation of the contract, an inconvenient and/or expensive situation for both parties. Protect your organization by not signing the contract until you know the ramifications of the technical requirements.

Differences
Between Disciplines

The vast philosophical and stylistic differences between theater and dance means the emphasis on production varies greatly. Presenters who are accustomed to producing plays are often amazed at the different needs and priorities of dance.

Since stages are normally designed to accommodate theatrical productions, most adapt readily to requirements of theater companies. Don't assume, however, that your theatre will accommodate any production you are contracting. Again, the best way to avoid problems is to anticipate them.

Dance

Rigging for dance varies radically. Some companies can get by with whatever is a standard house hang -- or the optimal placement of legs and borders which is left in place for most basic productions. Some companies prefer to perform in a bare stripped house, while other companies' productions rival any theatrical production in size and complexity. Since most dance is done in a repertory format there are often multiple quick scenic changes required between pieces, or sometimes within pieces. These quick changes of multiple scenic elements call for well-functioning rigging systems and quality fly crews. The glossary addresses rigging systems in some depth.

Presenters with a dead-hung house where there is no rigging system are faced with a whole new set of problems with dance in repertory. Some productions can adapt to a dead-hung facility, some can't.

Theater

Many theatrical productions, especially musical comedy and opera, use a vast number of flown set pieces and masking pieces requiring a fly system and many line sets. Be sure a company knows exactly how many line sets and battens (pipes hanging from the line sets) you have, where they're located on stage, and the height of your fly loft. If the company technicians know this information in advance, they can plan accurately where the flying elements will go, and if additional lines must be rigged, either you or the company can plan on procuring the necessary extra equipment. If you have battens that absolutely cannot be stripped, make it very clear to the company. If you tout the fact that your theatre has 75 line sets but only 35 are available or functioning, it makes an immense difference in the way a company approaches hanging their production. Be sure to remove all scenic elements stored in the fly loft in advance. This will save crew time and tempers during the set-up as well as possible damage to your scenery in the flys.

If you do not have a fly system, make sure that this fact is clear in the information you give out in advance prior to booking the company. Dead-hung houses pose a special problem unless the production is designed with elements supported off the ground. This ground-supported form of production tends to require large amounts of off-stage space for storage of these units. A dead-hung house with little storage space is doubly cursed!

LIGHTING

Dance

The most effective way to light the open space of a dance stage and to provide a maximum amount of definition to the body is to light from the sides of the stage in the wings. For this reason, side lighting is almost universal in dance production. Side lighting requires a tree or boom in each wing space with a number of instruments mounted on each. This form of lighting usually requires more Lekos, cable, and portable booms than many theatres own.

Since dance tends to minimize the use of scenic elements (especially modern dance), the demands on the lighting are maximized. Expect dance lighting designers to require much more -- and specific -- equipment than with theater. Dance usually uses more saturated colors of color media than does theater. Most dance companies will tend to carry their own color media for this reason.

Theater

Generally, lighting for theater tends to be softer and simpler than dance lighting. Expect to see the use of more Fresnels and floodlights on most theater light plots, and more traditional hanging positions than for dance. Color media tends to be softer tints and less specific.

SOUND

Dance

Music is an integral part of dance, yet very few companies travel with live musicians. Dance companies rely heavily on the quality of the sound system. The sound is usually on tape. Open reel machines are traditionally used for their ability to be cued up more easily than traditional cassettes. The advent of DAT (Digital Audio Tape) and its application in theatres will eventually revolutionize the abilities of audio tape, but DAT is just beginning to be utilized. If you are considering the purchase of a tape machine, thoroughly research commercial DAT machines.

Music for dance -- whether it is taped or live -- is usually *loud*. If a company travels with its own sound system (many do), it will not be of the quality or size of a professional permanent installation, and will not fill a large hall with the quality of sound often needed. Therefore, a presenter's quality sound system and top notch operator can substantially improve the sound reproduction for most dance companies.

Theater

As opposed to the needs of dance for music played at high levels, theater's prime need is for speech to be heard clearly at believably normal levels. Acoustics vary greatly from theatre to theatre, and the need for voice amplification will change according to the theatre acoustics. Almost any theatre sound system will be adequate for the sound of incidental music or special effects, but the effective reinforcement of the performer's voice -- when needed -- is terribly difficult and can at times evade even the best technicians with the best equipment. More and more companies are carrying their own wireless mikes with their own operators.

If your stage space is acoustically bad, or your sound system is less than reliable, inform the company well in advance. If they can supply their own sound system and technicians, the responsibility for sound amplification will be theirs. If you must rent a sound system, select the best possible one you can afford and check it out well in advance. Bugs in a sound system for either voice or tape can take many hours to trace, and bad sound can ruin a production faster than any other element of production.

Dance

Dancing is a dangerous business, and eliminating any possible hazard to the dancers is a full-time preoccupation of the company technicians. A clean stage is the first step. If a dancer steps on a stray nail or screw in some dark corner, he or she may be unable to dance for weeks. The elimination of obstacles backstage is also extremely important. There are enough objects in the way of the dancers with the side lights and the associated cable; extraneous items stored backstage are very dangerous.

An element that is commonly overlooked is the temperature of the stage. The dancers need to be warm to be able to move properly. The fact that they take class to warm-up, wear leg warmers, and stand in front of side lights is not enough. If the temperature on the stage is not at least seventy degrees, preferably closer to eighty, the dancers may not only be unable to dance properly, they may be in danger of seriously damaging a muscle or tendon. Rapid heating and cooling makes them susceptible to colds, bronchitis, and pneumonia. Raising the temperature is often a bother and a hassle, but it is worth the possible confrontation with the custodian when you consider the inherent danger to the dancers. The temperature of all support rooms and spaces the dancers use should be the same as the temperature on stage.

An open orchestra pit can be very dangerous to a disoriented dancer momentarily blinded by a black-out. A strip of phosphorescent tape at the edge of the apron can help. Nothing can guarantee that a performer won't tumble into the pit from a fall or freak accident. If a person were to fall into an empty pit, he or she would be hurt much less than if the pit were full of debris.

FLOOR

Dance

To some presenters the floor is a floor, and not a priority. This is a misconception. The entire floor -- the sub-floor, the support structure, and the surface layer -- is critical to most performing art forms. The floor is the least adaptable of all elements of a stage. A floor that works optimally for theater or opera is not a floor that works well for dance. And since a bad floor surface or subsurface construction can be career-threatening for a dancer, the floor can become the most problematic element of a theatre facility.

The traditional floor for theater productions is purposefully *not* resilient so that large wagon platforms remain stable when rolled across the stage. The floor is often trapped or elevatored for flexibility of staging and is preferably constructed of a soft wood such as pine or fir that is much more self-healing when penetrated by a screw or nail than hardwood surfaces. This floor is the antithesis of a good safe floor for dance.

Dance Floor Needs

There are several separate but critical needs for a dance floor: resilience, floor covering, surface condition, and storage.

■ **Resilience**: A floor designed specifically for theater productions will not normally be built with a resilient subsurface. Resilience is a crucial requirement in any floor that is to be used for dance. If the floor does not provide a certain amount of spring or resilience, dancers can be seriously injured by merely performing on it. Damage can range all the way from very common but painful shin splints to broken bones that can end a dancer's career. Non-resilient floors are typically wood supported directly on concrete or metal piers with no leeway for the movement of the floor.

A resilient dance floor is best made of wood construction with a basket weave of wood supports (or sleepers) positioned so that there is not a point on the surface that directly touches the base slab. A common practice among architects today is to lay a floor surface on neoprene rubber cushions or isolators. This makes a fine floor for aerobics but, in my biased opinion, is only marginally acceptable for dance.

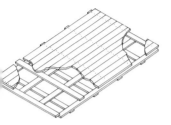

Cross-section of a basket weave sub-floor

If you ever are in a situation to build a stage floor to accommodate dance, build a basket weave sub-floor. Don't reinvent the wheel! Although it won't have traps and it will flex when heavy wagons roll over it, a basket weave floor is the best, safest, and often cheapest form of floor that can be installed in a theatre for multiple purposes.

You should be able to tell if there is any spring or resilience to the floor by simply jumping on it. If you're in doubt, bring in a dancer and have him or her jump for a while. All dancers react against non-resilient floors, but some are more demanding than others. If your floor is non-resilient or barely resilient, let the company know before contracts are signed. There are temporary ways to add resilience to a floor. One method is very effective and expensive, others are neither. We'll start at the bottom end.

In an emergency situation where the floor is awful (i.e., brick, tile, grass, or lava flow) and if the performer is not terribly fussy, it is possible to lay approximately two inches of resilient building board like Celotex or Homosote covered with battleship linoleum or Masonite and a vinyl dance floor. Another emergency subsurface is two inches of Styrofoam building board covered with battleship or masonite and vinyl. Its use is not normally recommended since its extreme flammability makes it illegal or unsafe in many applications.

In the early 1980's a new portable, temporary sub-floor was introduced called D'Anser. It was originally marketed through Rosco Labs but is now sold exclusively through its manufacturer, Oasis Stage Werks in Salt Lake City, Utah. It is a true basket weave sprung dance floor built in 4 foot x 8 foot sections that can be installed and or removed in a matter of hours (or minutes if you have enough bodies). It is a wonderful floor used by many of the top ballet companies in the United States. Its major drawback is its cost. At about $10 a square foot it is an expensive solution but one that can be very effective and less expensive than building a completely new stage floor. D'Anser is also very effective for dance studios which lease space and require a non-permanent resilient floor. Storage can be a problem since it does require a large, dry storage space when not in use.

■ **Floor Covering**: The issue of floor covering is easier to address. A wooden stage floor -- either of a soft wood that tends to splinter terribly or a hard wood that is slick and distractingly reflective -- is not an acceptable surface for dancers and must be covered with an appropriate material to make it into a dance floor.

Permanent installation: The only permanent stage floor that is acceptable for dance is that one-in-fifty that is covered with battleship linoleum. Battleship linoleum is a good surface for dance as long as it is scrupulously clean and free from holes and paint. Old fashioned battleship linoleum has resurfaced since its demise in 1974. It is imported from Scandinavia by a company called Forbo North America Inc. It has all the benefits and vices of the old battleship. It is heavy, brittle and lasts forever if it is put in a permanent installation and treated with some care. I would never suggest battleship for a temporary installation but for a permanent installation on a stage or studio, it's the best compromise for a general purpose, permanent installation. It comes in two weights (I prefer the heavier Krommenie Plain Linoleum) and sixteen colors.

Non-permanent installation: There is a simple solution for the floor covering dilemma. In the early 1970's an English product was introduced into the United States called a Marley floor. The Marley is a very thin vinyl flooring (much like a drawing board cover) that comes in rolls. It is rolled out and taped down whenever dance is performed on the stage, thus covering splinters and floor irregularities and giving a consistent surface for the dancer. Marley has long since gone out of business, but its descendants remain and flourish and are much better than the once revolutionary Marley. The name Marley, however, remains and is -- like Xerox to copiers -- still in common use throughout North America.

If I have to pick a current favorite for a portable vinyl floor that is great for ballet and seems to be preferred by many modern dancers, it would have to be the Studio floor by Harlequin. It is a medium weight with foam backing. It is long-lived and durable, and its backing helps keep it from deforming over the years. Its surface is lauded by most dancers, and its dark grey color is an appropriate compromise for most staging situations.

When laying any portable floor, the seams should be taped to keep the performer from tripping on them. Some companies use double-faced tape underneath the floor, but this is time consuming, expensive and still can offer an edge of flooring to trip on. The easiest way to lay a floor is to tape it on the face. Leave a space of 1/4 inch between the rolls of floor as you lay it on the stage. This allows the floor to expand without buckling once it heats and also allows the tape to grip the stage surface to stabilize the floor. Some companies prefer to use gaffer's tape, a black, matte-surfaced tape two inches wide, while some prefer to use two-inch aisle marking tape, a shiny vinyl tape that comes in a variety of colors including a clear tape that disappears on the surface and lets the color of the flooring show through. Choose a tape that leaves no adhesive residue and matches the surface of the floor. Theatrical supply houses carry a variety of tape sizes and colors; many of these suppliers have catalogs.

Sources: In the first edition of this handbook, written in 1975, I listed several manufacturers of portable floor coverings. Within four years all of those types of floor mentioned were out of manufacture. There are currently three prime manufacturers of portable floor coverings (the aerobics boom created enormous new markets for flooring). Each of these manufacturers make different types of flooring for specific applications. Some are light and easy to transport, while some are heavy and possibly more durable. Some are stiff and work well for extended installations, while other more pliable types lay and store more easily. Some surfaces are preferred for aerobics, ballet, or modern dance. There is not one best universal floor. Each of the companies presently making portable dance floors are making products far superior to the old Marley. Unlike fifteen years ago, dance floors are not hard to find. Listed below are the addresses for the main office of each company. They will be able to give you the names of local distributors.

Portable:

Harlequin
3111 West Burbank Boulevard
Burbank, California 91505
(800) 642-6440

Stage-Step
PO Box 328
Philadelphia, Pennsylvania 19105
(800) 523-0961

Rosco Labs
36 Bush Avenue
Port Chester, New York 10573
(914) 937-1300

D'Anser/Oasis Stage Werks
263 S. Rio Grande Street
Salt Lake City, Utah 84101
(801) 363-0364

Permanent:

Forbo North America, Inc.
P.O. Box 32155
Richmond, Virginia 23294
(800)-233-0475

■ **Surface condition**: Once the type of floor covering has been determined, it is necessary to cope with the problem of the condition of the surface. The sticky floor versus slippery floor fight will never be completely resolved. Ballet dancers normally prefer much stickier floors than modern dancers. A ballet dancer on pointe needs a sticky floor to stay on pointe. A floor that is too sticky will tear up the bare feet of a modern dancer. Often dancers in the same company can't agree among themselves as to whether the surface is right. Because of this, they have developed their own ways of correcting the surface. Ballet dancers use rosin to give their shoes more friction. Modern dancers use glycerin or Coca-Cola to give stick and talcum powder to give slip.

However, the most important aspect of the surface is that it must be smooth and free of splinters, holes, or protrusions like screws, nails, or staples. These can literally rip the feet of a dancer to shreds. Taping over a bad surface presents a problem as it becomes a protrusion with a very different amount of friction than the rest of the floor. It is quite possible for a dancer to trip over a patch of tape on the floor.

The appearance of the surface is also a factor. Since the settings for dance are often minimal, the visual impact of the stage itself is very important. If the floor is covered with tape or paint splatters, it can be very distracting. In addition, the lighter the floor itself is, the more light is reflected onto the backdrops. A very light, bright floor will also diminish the visual impact of the dancers by lessening the contrast between the performer and his surroundings. These problems are most easily cured by the use of a portable floor covering which can cover flaws and still be removed to allow the use of nails and paint for theater productions. Even though some companies travel with their own portable floor covering, a portable floor is well worth the investment if you present dance on a regular basis.

A gymnasium floor usually offers very good resilience and a danceable surface. Keep in mind, though, that ballet companies need to use rosin, which is usually not allowed on gym floors. The largest problem with performing on a gym floor is one of aesthetics. The pale color is very difficult to light and the lines are distracting. A dark portable dance floor covering on a gym does wonders for defining the space and helping the overall effect.

Dance Floor Storage

Once you own a portable floor covering, its care and storage is critical. Most manufacturers will suggest that floors be rolled around a core of some sort. After over twenty years of dealing with portable floors, I have found that what is critical is not whether the floor has a core but whether the floor has been stored vertically, on its end. Storage of a roll of floor on its side, even for a few hours, can do more damage to a floor than years of vertical storage. When a floor is laid on its side in a roll, it will flatten and deform, even if has a core in the center. This deformation of the roll -- which creates a wavy effect when laid -- can become permanent very quickly and ruin a very valuable investment. *Keep the floor stored vertically!* This is little insurance to pay for a floor that has cost you thousands of dollars.

The best form of storage for a vinyl floor is a six foot length of twelve inch Sonotube concrete form for each piece of floor. (Sonotube is manufactured for the construction industry and is readily available from concrete specialty firms.) Attach a plywood round in one end of each roll of Sonotube. When you are taking the floor up, roll it as tightly as possible. When the roll is completed, tape the floor to itself so that it stays rolled. Stand it on one end and drop the Sonotube over the roll of floor. Then, gently, tip the roll of floor and the Sonotube over and then upright on the closed end. The floor will now be protected by the Sonotube and can easily moved to storage on an appliance dolly.

Theater

In theater, as in dance, the floor poses a problem. Theater productions often require that screws or nails be driven into the floor to secure set pieces. Some building managers with polished wood floors flatly refuse to let anyone drive screws or nails into them. It is a ridiculous policy to refuse to allow a stage to be used properly as a stage, but it does happen very frequently. This is an item that does need to be addressed before contracts are signed.

There is an alternative acceptable to some building managers. In some circumstances it is possible to use "improved stage screws" or "Patent Pegs." These use a female threaded insert which is sunk into the floor to receive the stage screw, or "Patent Peg." After the production the insert is removed with a screw driver and the hole is filled with a hard wood dowel which is sawed off flush with the floor. The company may carry these "Patent Pegs;" if not, presenters can obtain them from theatrical supply sources.

Heavy theatrical wagons can have nearly as much problem with an uneven, splintered stage floor as a dancer. It is the presenter's responsibility to keep any stage floor in good repair.

What Does It Mean?
A Glossary of Terms

This is not a standard glossary in alphabetical order. It has been broken down into categories, then items have been addressed more or less in their order of importance. This section is really an opportunity to discuss the different elements of production and look at some potential problem areas.

The first section will deal with stage directions and terminology used for basic technological communication. The second section addresses stage rigging and fly systems. The third section deals with masking and draperies. The fourth section describes the instrument mounting positions. The final section goes into some depth describing stage electrical equipment.

Directions

In the theatre, lateral directions are given in terms of **stage left** and **stage right**. This is the performer's left and right as he or she faces the audience and is the orientation used by technicians. **Upstage** and **downstage** are terms that originated in the time of raked stages when the back of the stage floor was slanted higher than the front. Thus the portion of the stage closest to the audience is downstage, and the back of the stage is upstage. **House left** and **house right** are terms used by box office and house staffs, and refer to the right/left orientation of the audience member facing the stage.

Proscenium Arch

The proscenium arch is the opening in the downstage wall separating the audience and the stage. In older theatres the proscenium is usually a true architectural arch, often highly decorated. More recent architectural practice has been to minimize the proscenium to the point that the actual arch may be simple movable panels or only draperies.

Fly Loft

The fly loft (or fly gallery) is the space directly above the stage area where draperies and lighting instruments are hung. Ideally, the height of the fly loft is three times as high as the proscenium arch to allow for the scenic elements to be flown out of sight. From the outside of the building the fly loft is that huge rectangular block of masonry that identifies most theatres in the world as theatres. Due to either economic or aesthetic factors, many people who build theatres -- but never have to use them -- see fit to reduce the size of the fly loft or to eliminate it entirely. For most forms of production this is a deadly omission. If your theatre claims to be a proscenium theatre but has a height-to-proscenium ratio of less than three to one, be sure and let a prospective company know, since it can greatly inhibit their ability to produce properly.

Grid

The grid is the metal framework at the top of the fly loft or just below the stage roof. Consider it as the ceiling of the fly loft. Everything that hangs or flies on the stage is suspended from the grid. When a company asks about the height of the grid, they usually want to know how far out (or how high) the battens fly.

Dead-Hung

Many theatres do not have a fly loft or the ability to fly equipment and scenery in and out. Instead of a grid, there are non-movable (or dead-hung) pipes. To hang or remove instruments, you must climb up to the pipes (rather than bringing them to the deck or stage as with a fly system).

Stage or Deck

The stage or deck is the entire floor of the theatre inside the stage house under the grid. The term **"on stage"** denotes that area of the stage that is visible to the audience. The term **"off stage"** is that area hidden from the view of the audience.

Apron

The apron of a stage is that area of the floor that extends through the proscenium arch towards the audience.

Wing

The wing is the area off stage hidden from the view of the audience by masking. A wing is a space, not a drapery.

Plaster Line

The plaster line is the primary reference point for determining measurements up and down stage. It is a line drawn across the stage at the upstage edge of the proscenium. For instance, if the upstage corner of the set is listed on the paperwork as being 33 feet 6 inches, it means that the corner is 33 feet 6 inches upstage of the plaster line. It is the determiner of the downstage limit of the stage separating the stage from the apron.

Curtain Line

The curtain line is a term similar to the plaster line, in that it is a reference point for measuring up and down stage. It is not as accurate a measurement as the plaster line, however, since the act curtain can measure anywhere from a foot to two feet wide at the bottom, and heating and air conditioning can make it shift as much as four feet. The plaster line is the preferred measurement to use.

Center Line

The center line is the major reference line for measuring laterally on stage. It is the line running directly down the middle of the stage separating stage left from stage right. All measurements on the stage are made up and down from the plaster line and left and right from the center line.

Ground Plan

The ground plan (often just called a plan) is an aerial view of the stage drawn to a specific scale (usually one-quarter inch equals one foot or one-half inch equals one foot) showing all the pertinent elements of the stage. It is a prime tool of theatre technicians for planning productions and communicating stage information with one another. Every theatre should have an accurate ground plan that should be included in any technical communications. (Don't use the architect's plans that were used to build the building. These don't have the proper information needed by technicians. "As built" and "as designed" are often two different things.)

Section

A section is a side view of the stage as seen through the middle of the stage. This is not a required drawing, but can be very valuable for larger, more complex facilities. Its primary value is to allow a designer or technician to see if the show will mask. To mask a show is to hide all extraneous elements from the audience using a combination of the scenic elements, legs, and borders.

Light Plot

A light plot is a plan view of the stage with the lighting instruments superimposed showing where each is hung, what type it is, what dimmer it is patched into, what circuit it is plugged into, and what color it is gelled. Some light plots are drawn directly over a ground plan of the stage, while some are drawn in a schematic style and not necessarily done to the scale of the stage. The light plot is provided by the company's lighting designer to the presenter.

Hanger Log

A hanger log (often called a hanging schedule or hanger sheet) is a document describing the location of each line set in a rigging system (see below). This is a critical document. The presenter generates the base hanger log. It shows not only the number of the line set, but its distance upstage from the plaster line and any specifics impacting the use of those lines, i.e.: how long are the battens, how far out do the battens fly, what items are permanently hung on which battens, and what is traditionally hung on battens to best mask the house (lines usually reserved for legs and borders). Any oddity of the fly system should be stated here, such as lines that won't fly all the way out, bent battens, or clearance problems.

In listing battens that cannot be stripped, remember that there is a difference between items that can't be moved and items that are inconvenient to move or remove. Some technicians don't ever like to take their lighting instruments or draperies off the pipes. For some small touring companies traveling without any equipment or scenery this may not be an inconvenience, but for a large production carrying its own lighting and scenery it can be cause for cancellation of a contract. If a company's tech rider requires a stripped house before load-in, they mean it. In a situation like this the safest place for your drapes and lighting instruments is off the stage and in storage.

Once the company receives the hanger log from the presenter, the company's technical director will fill out the company's requirements on the log and return it to the presenter. This gives the presenter's technical director an indication of what will be moving into the theatre. It is this technical director's responsibility to read the completed log and react to any potential problems.

Since it is impossible to fly the battens in a dead-hung house, it is all the more important to find a creative way to describe what is available and possible to do in your theatre. An accurate diagram of the battens or grid-work is usually a helpful tool. Since the height of the battens can't be changed, it is crucial to know exactly what that height is. With a dead-hung stage, factors we tend to take for granted on a traditional stage -- like the diameter and weight of the pipes themselves or the breaking strength of the chain, cable, rope, or pipe clamps that support those pipes -- becomes very important. Some dead-hung houses are well-engineered and well-designed; some are not and may actually be a safety hazard. A full electric batten or a large velour drape can weigh more than a thousand pounds. If the battens are hung with a simple dog chain (as many of them are), they are completely unsafe and shouldn't be used. Many dead-hung houses don't even have battens for the draperies, but have useless lightweight aluminum tracks.

RIGGING SYSTEMS

Stage rigging is a misunderstood and potentially dangerous form of machinery. All presenters need to know at least a little about that tangle of rope and cable dangling over their heads.

Systems

The rigging or fly system is a series of cables, pulleys, and counterweight-filled arbors that enable scenery, drapes, or lighting equipment to fly in and out. This ability to make scenery change almost instantly is what helps create the "magic of theatre." There are three basic types of fly systems.

■ **Hemp or Sandbag**: The hemp or sandbag system is the oldest and, these days, rarest, of the available types of rigging. It uses hemp ropes to support the battens, and the scenic elements attached to them. The batten is counterbalanced by several large sandbags. This is a very old system but can work well in the hands of a competent flyman (who is rarer than the system). Many modern theatres will use a few sandbag lines to augment their regular systems.

■ **Synchronous winch**: The second, newest style of rigging system is one using synchronous winches to lift the battens. This approach has worked with very mixed results in a limited number of theatres around the country. The idea has merit, but the winches have myriad inherent problems, and very few installations work flawlessly the way a rigging system needs to work.

■ **Counterweight**: The most common rigging system is called the counterweight system. The battens are supported by metal aircraft cable, and the counterbalances are steel or iron counterweights held in a large metal arbor. Since this is the system used in 95% of all theatres, we will explore it in more depth below.

Line Set

The term line set describes a single working group of elements that enables scenery or lighting equipment to move up and down or to "fly." A pipe is attached by cables and pulleys to a counterweight arbor placed against the stage wall. When the arbor is pulled toward the stage, the pipe (or batten) moves toward the grid or "flies out." When the arbor is pulled toward the grid, the pipe (or batten) moves toward the stage floor or "flies in." A group of line sets creates a fly system. In describing the elements of the system, I'll start at one end of the line set and work to the other. Fifty to sixty line sets is common for a moderately large theatre, while some stages get up to the range of 100-120. Line sets are usually evenly spaced up and down stage on 6, 8 or 9-inch centers.

■ **Batten**: A batten is a horizontal steel pipe attached to the cables of the fly system. All scenery and lighting equipment is tied or clamped to the battens. Preferably a batten will be approximately 20 feet longer than the width of the proscenium (i.e., a 40-foot proscenium would have 60-foot battens). Battens were originally made of wood and adapted from battens on sailing ships. In fact, a major portion of theatrical rigging design and terminology came directly from the rigging of sailing ships.

■ **Lift lines**: The lift lines are the steel aircraft cables that support the batten. Each line set will use anywhere from three to nine lift lines depending on the size of the batten. The lift lines then run to the grid and are supported by the sheaves in the loftblocks and the headblocks.

■ **Sheave**: The sheave (pronounced "shiv") is actually the pulley portion of a loftblock or headblock, but in common use it is the term often used to describe loftblocks and headblocks.

■ **Loftblock**: A loftblock is the single sheave unit mounted on the grid as a support for each single lift line run.

- **Headblock**: A headblock is the group of three to nine sheaves mounted together as a single unit where all the lift lines from a single batten come together. The headblock is mounted to a steel beam (called the headblock beam) at the side wall of the stage house above the area where the line sets are operated.
- **Floorblock**: A floorblock or tension block is a single block mounted on the stage floor (or sometimes below stage level) that redirects the endless line back toward the headblock on the grid.
- **Arbors**: After the lift lines go over the loftblock and the headblock they head down the stagehouse wall and are attached to an arbor. The arbor is a rectangular steel carriage designed to hold counterweights. Depending on the size of the theatre an arbor will be from five to twelve feet long, and hold from 600 to 2000 pounds of steel counterweights. It is guided in its travel up and down the stagehouse wall by either Tee-track guides or wire-guides.
- **Tee-track**: Tee-track is a steel latticework of parallel bars used to guide and control the arbor. This is the preferred type of arbor guide for all medium and large theatres.
- **Wire-guide**: Wire-guides are parallel aircraft cables running through holes on the edges of the arbor and stretched between the grid and the stage. They are a much cheaper, less efficient, and more dangerous form of guiding the arbor travel. This system is acceptable in small theatres with few line sets and low grid height.
- **Endless line**: Attached at the bottom of each arbor there is a rope, usually 5/8-inch to 3/4-inch manila hemp. This is the actual rope that is pulled by the operator (called a flyman) that makes the system work. The endless line (often called the rope, purchase line, or line) runs from the bottom of the arbor to the stage deck where it runs around another sheave on a floorblock or tension block. The endless line then runs directly back up to the grid, over the same headblock that supports the lift lines, and down to the arbor where it is attached at the top of the arbor this time. This is why it is called an endless line, since it becomes a circle of rope with the arbor attached in the middle. Therefore, when the flyman pulls on the back side of the endless line (the one attached to the bottom of the arbor and furthest away from the operator), the arbor flies (travels) in (toward the stage) and the batten flies out (toward the grid). When the flyman pulls on the front side of the endless line, the arbor flies out and the batten flies in.

    Very simple and effective, yes, but very dangerous. We are dealing with thousands of pounds of weight moving in and out above the performers' heads. As productions change, the weights have to change, and the potential for battens and arbors getting out of control is enormous. A line set flies smoothly only as long as the arbor is correctly counterweighted. If an arbor is "out of weight" it can be a deadly missile.
- **Locking rail and rope lock**: The endless line passes through a locking mechanism called a rope lock which is mounted on a steel bar called a locking rail. The locking rail is sometimes mounted on the stage floor and sometimes mounted on a pinrail, or working platform, built several feet above the stage floor to preserve stage space or allow for openings in the wall for doors or alcoves. This is the place where the flyman operates the system.
- **Loading platform**: A platform or catwalk built near the grid in front of the arbors is called a loading platform or loading dock. It is the position from which the arbors are loaded or counterweighted.

Single purchase/double purchase

There are two variations of the counterweight rigging system that are quite different in their impact on a production. The system that I have described above is called a single purchase system. This means that there is a one-to-one mechanical ratio with the endless line. The batten travels one foot for each foot that the arbor travels.

The double purchase system adds a second sheave at the bottom of the arbor where the endless line travels through and back down to the floorblock. With this system the batten travels two feet for every one foot that the arbor travels since the added sheave gives an added mechanical advantage (double purchase). This system allows the floorblock to be mounted on the pinrail rather than on the stage floor, thus freeing up the lower portion of the stage wall for doors, alcoves, storage or whatever. This style has many advantages on paper for architects looking for space or gimmicks. To anyone who has ever actually worked a show from a pinrail it is a disaster. The two-to-one mechanical advantage becomes a two-to-one weight disadvantage. This means that if a large scenic wall weighs 900 pounds, the weight loader must add 1800 pounds of counterweight. This is an extremely slow process and opens the door for even more danger of a mis-loaded arbor. There is an incredible amount of added inertia in a double purchase system making the process of getting the arbor moving and, more importantly, getting it stopped very difficult. The rope also travels twice as far in a double purchase system making any pull of a rope twice as long for the flyman.

With many productions the quality of the fly system is not a factor, but when a large show with many scenic elements moves into your facility and the company must make that show work with little or no rehearsal, the quality of the fly system can become the single most important element of your theatre. If you ever have a chance to be involved in the construction or renovation of a theatre, please fight for a single purchase system. Many theatres get a reputation of having an inept and slow fly crew. Before accusing the crew, the rigging system should be examined since the best flyman in the world can look like a fool with a double purchase system.

Trim

The distance measured between the deck and a batten indicating the height of that batten when it is in a working position is called the trim height.

MASKING AND DRAPES

Any drapery or scenic piece used to define the stage or impede the view of the audience is called masking. Masking terminology is an area with a great deal of duplication and incorrect application of terms.

Border

A border is a horizontal drape used to control the area of the stage seen by the audience and hide from view items in the fly loft such as lighting equipment and scenery.

Leg

A vertical masking piece hung at the sides of the stage used to hide the wing spaces and define the width of the stage. A series of legs and borders is the most common form of masking for dance.

Wing

The offstage space between the legs.

Grand Drape

The first (downstage) border; often very ornamental in older theatres. It is the visual determiner of the height of the proscenium opening (called the trim height). It is not the main curtain that opens and closes.

Tormentor or Torm

The first (downstage) leg. It can be a soft drapery but is often framed and solid. This is the first visual determiner of the width of the stage.

Teaser

The term teaser is used to define the first horizontal masking piece. Used in conjunction with a tormentor, this first masking set of the tormentor and teaser becomes what is often called a portal. What is really a grand drape and what is a teaser is a grey area. In rigid definition, the tormentor and the teaser are the first framed, masking pieces used as a set to form a portal. Occasionally a theatre will have both a grand drape and a teaser. All horizontal masking pieces are not teasers; only the first piece is a teaser (the rest are borders), unless it's a grand drape. See how simple!

Act Curtain or House Curtain

The act curtain is the curtain that opens and closes, separating the audience from the stage. It is usually hung directly upstage of the grand drape. It can either open in the center (called traveling), or it can fly in and out (called guillotining).

Asbestos or Fire Curtain

A fire-resistant curtain located at the proscenium opening immediately downstage of the act curtain. For most stages it is required by law. Since asbestos is now illegal, it has been replaced by fiberglass woven fabrics. The most common brand name is Zee-tex. Often a small border of asbestos (Zee-tex) is hung on an electric to keep lighting instruments from burning draperies.

Cyclorama

A cyclorama (usually just called a cyc) is a very large fabric drop rigged at the back of the stage, with curved arms wrapping downstage enclosing the stage. It was designed to create sky effects and to give a feeling of great depth. A true wrap around cyc is usually not applicable for dance as the downstage curved portion provides a barrier that makes exits and side-lighting very difficult or impossible.

Sky Drop

A sky drop is a flat fabric drop at the back of the stage used for sky effects without wrapping downstage like a cyclorama. It is sometimes referred to as a cyc.

Scrim

A transparent gauze material used for stage effects such as ghosts, clouds, or any effect requiring something to appear and disappear. When lit from the front, it becomes opaque; when back lit, it becomes transparent. A scrim is often used in front of a skydrop to give more sense of depth. The most common fabric for a scrim is called sharkstooth; other fabrics are opera net or bobinette.

INSTRUMENT MOUNTING POSITIONS

Any dimmable lighting fixture on the stage is called a lighting instrument. The lighting instruments are clamped to a pipe. This pipe is then called an electrical mounting position. Any pipe anywhere can be a mounting position for temporary situations, but the term mounting position refers to a pipe specifically mounted for hanging lighting instruments. This pipe will usually have an electrical raceway called a connector strip bolted to or adjacent to it with multiple dimmable circuits inside the strip. Some mounting positions are permanent, while others are portable. Mounting positions, especially in the front of house, can change from theatre to theatre. This variation in mounting positions can make the job of lighting a touring show in a short period of time very tricky.

Electric

An electric (or electric batten) is an on-stage batten with cable and connectors mounted on it specifically used for hanging instruments. The electric can fly in and out with the other battens in the fly system. Electrics can be parallel to the proscenium like most of the fly system, or they can be perpendicular to the proscenium mounted at the sides of the stage. These are called side electrics and are most often used for dance. The term electric is also used in dead-hung houses.

Bridge

Bridge is the term used for an electric constructed from a large truss-work instead of the simple batten. The bridge was originally designed so a stagehand could move about on it to adjust the carbons of early carbon-arc spotlights.

Boom

A vertical pipe used for mounting lighting instruments. **On-stage booms** are usually portable. The terms tree, tower, and ladder are often used as variations for portable boom. When mounted in the auditorium, they are usually a permanent fixture. **House booms** are permanent booms mounted to the auditorium wall. **Box booms** are mounted in or on a box seat. **Balcony booms** are mounted in the balcony.

F.O.H. (Front of House)

Any mounting position in the auditorium.

A.P. (Ante-Pro)

A mounting position in the auditorium between the proscenium and the edge of the apron or -- like F.O.H. -- any mounting position in front of the proscenium.

Balcony Rail

A mounting position on the front edge of the balcony. Some theatres have multiple balcony rail positions on their multiple balconies. Most balcony rail positions are so low that the lighting angle is low and unflattering, and is often of limited value.

Beam Slot

The beam slot is the term used for any horizontal ceiling mounting position parallel to the proscenium. This position got its name from the practice of building the auditorium with the ceiling mounting positions concealed within a decorative beam with a slot cut in the upstage edge. There are a number of conflicting terms used for this position. Some people call them coves, some call them catwalks, and some simply call them slots.

Coves

Many houses will have a permanent boom built into the side walls of the auditorium. These, again, have myriad conflicting names such as cove, flipper, cheek, side slit, etc.

LIGHTING EQUIPMENT

Most aspects of theatre have changed very little over the years, especially the architecture and the mechanical elements. For the most part this is good. A traditional space with traditional rigging is, by far, the preferred facility for most touring performers. The one area where technology has invaded, and vastly improved, the theatre has been in lighting. There have been monumental strides in stage lighting over the past twenty years, and a theatre untouched by lighting equipment advances since the sixties is truly a dinosaur.

The general name for any dimmable lighting fixture that is specifically designed for stage use is called a lighting instrument. Here, again, the terminology gets pretty muddled. A lighting instrument can be called a light or an instrument. It isn't proper to call an instrument a lamp, though, since the lamp is the glass and tungsten unit (what you call a light bulb) that creates the light within the instrument. There are two general groups of lighting instruments: spotlights and floodlights. These terms are rarely used without specific qualification.

Spotlights

Spotlights are, by far, the most common group of theatre instruments. A spotlight is differentiated from a floodlight by the fact that it uses a lens in front of the lamp to shape the beam of light and direct it in a specific pattern, or spot of light. The floodlight has no lens and therefore emits a soft wash, or flood of light. There are two major types of spotlights: Ellipsoidal Reflector Spotlights and Fresnels. Between them, these two types account for ninety percent of all normally used instruments.

■ **Fresnel** ("fre-nel"): The full name of this instrument is Fresnel-lens spotlights, named after Dr. Fresnel who invented the lens for lighthouses. Fresnel is this instrument's only correct name, but terms such as juniors, coffee grinders, or inkies are common slang usually used to specify a certain size. Fresnels come in several sizes which are measured by the diameter of the lens. Six and eight-inch lenses are the most common, although Fresnels are manufactured all the way

Fresnel
Strand Lighting

from three inches to thirty inches. A Fresnel gives a wide beam, soft-edged light that does certain lighting jobs very well. An even, patternless wash of the stage from overhead is best handled by Fresnels as they blend with one another very well. The beam of light cannot be shaped well, and this greatly limits the use of Fresnels from positions where precise beam control is needed. A common accessory for a Fresnel is a unit called a barn door. These are movable blades affixed to the front of a Fresnel that allows the beam of light to be shaped slightly and kept off the background or audience. There are several companies manufacturing Fresnels and, since they are quite simple in their design, most are of similar quality.

■ **Ellipsoidal Reflector Spotlights/Lekos** ("lee-ko"): This is the most commonly used type of instrument in the theatre today. It goes by many names in many areas. The name ERS was used early on but hasn't seemed to stick. Most commonly they are called simply an ellipsoidal; sometimes they are called by their lens specifications (i.e., a 6 x 9, a 6 x 12, a 40 degree, a 10 degree and so on). Often they are called Lekos. Leko is an acronym of the names of the two men who developed the instrument: Mr. Levy and Mr. Kook. Although technically incorrect, the name Leko has become the generic name and is as commonly used for an ellipsoidal as the name Kleenex is for tissue. The name Leko was first marketed by the Lighting Corporation of America, later to become Century, then Strand-Century, then Rank-Strand, now just called Strand Lighting. Therefore, Strand lighting's brand of ERS is, correctly, called a Lekolite.

Ellipsoidal Reflector Spotlight (Leko)
Strand Lighting

The Leko is the work-horse of all instruments. They are the most powerful, the most efficient, and the most flexible of all stage lighting instruments. The combination of an ellipsoidal reflector and double plano-convex lenses gives the Leko a hard-edged beam of light that can be easily shaped and controlled to allow the light to be focused where it's needed and cut off of any object that shouldn't be illuminated, such as a leg or the proscenium arch. They can have patterns, called **gobos** or **templates**, inserted into them that can shape the light to any outline, projecting any shape from trees, to stars, to skylines of Manhattan.

There are complexities, however, that make dealing with a Leko difficult. On a Fresnel the beam of light can be adjusted from a wide beam to a narrow spot. The Leko, on the other hand, has a fixed beam spread. The size of the beam remains roughly the same even though the edges can be made hard or somewhat soft. To achieve a different beam spread (larger or smaller), it is necessary to change the lenses to a different focal-length lens system. There are two numbers used in designating any Leko: the first is the diameter of the lens (as with the Fresnel), and the second is the focal length used. The longer the focal length, the narrower the beam. Therefore, a 6 x 9 Lekolite would have a lens diameter of six inches and a focal length of nine inches, and would be considered a wide beam spread instrument. A 6 x 12 Lekolite would look like a 6 x 9 on the outside but would have a narrow beam and a more intense light. As the design of ellipsoidals have become more sophisticated over the last few years, manufacturers have begun to designate their instruments by the degree of beam spread. Therefore it has become common to see instruments designated as 40 degree, 30 degree, 20 degree and so on. Several years ago zoom lensed ellipsoidals were introduced and are now gaining a certain amount of popularity. Their light isn't quite as good as a fixed-lens ellipsoidal, but the ability to change the beam spread without changing the lens barrel is very appealing to many institutions. Lekos are very expensive. They cannot be substituted for effectively, and dance designers use them extensively. Some designers use them exclusively.

Floodlights

Floodlights are the other major sub-group of instruments. The primary difference between spotlights and floodlights is the lens. Since the floodlight doesn't have a lens, it does not allow for any change or modification of the beam spread. They are a very simple instrument designed to give an even wash of light.

■ **Border striplight**: The very first type of incandescent stage lighting was a form of floodlight known as a border striplight. It was nothing but a long sheet metal trough filled with a row of small wattage, household type "A" lamps. It gave illumination to the stage much the way fluorescent tubes illuminate a modern office space. There are still derivations of the original borderstrip in use today, usually called either a striplight or a borderlight. Their only real purpose in lighting dance is for lighting back-drops and cycloramas. In theatre they are used occasionally for toning and blending on the stage. Striplights have recently staged a comeback for lighting drops and cycloramas. Modern units with double-ended tungsten halogen lamps and sophisticated reflectors have become common for cyc lighting applications (especially when mounted on the floor to light the bottom of the cyc).

A recent trend toward miniaturization has been spearheaded by the use of the MR-16 lamp. This low-voltage lamp is only the size of a pea. It is enclosed by its own reflector and is incredibly bright for its size. The MR-16 (for mirrored reflector, 16/8" or two inches in diameter), has been tried in many types of miniaturized instruments. The most successful application of the MR-16 has been in what are commonly called mini-strips. Utilizing strings of low-voltage MR-16s in series, the mini-strip is able to emit enormous amounts of smooth wash light while being housed in a sleek shape only about four inches wide.

■ **Footlights**: Footlights are rarely, if ever, used in dance because exposed footlights are hazardous to dancers. They are occasionally used for theater productions. Footlights have some application for scenic toning and can be useful at low level for musicals, opaquing downstage scrims, and as curtain warmers.

■ **Scoops/Far-Cyc**: The type of floodlight in most common use today is the high wattage single unit flood. The older style of this type is called a scoop. It is nothing more than a spherical reflector with a large A-type lamp of 750 to 1000 watts. The scoop has been replaced by what is generally called a far-cyc. Like the newer generation of striplights, the far-cyc uses a double-ended tungsten halogen lamp of 1000 to 1500 watts. Its reflector is a sophisticated variable curve that evenly distributes light over the entire surface of a drop.

■ **Follow spots**: A follow spot is a spot that can move or follow performers. It can simply be a modification of a Leko, or it can be a very high-powered xenon-arc lamp. It gets little use in modern dance or theater but is quite common in ballet and musical comedy. The most current generation of follow spots are much smaller and more efficient than the old carbon-arc monster of the past. Follow spots are highly adjustable as to the size and softness of the beam, but the skill of the operator is crucial. A bad follow spot operator can ruin any performance. Because of that, the decision to use a follow spot on a touring production should hinge on the quality of the operators.

- **PAR lamps**: A PAR is a stamped sheetsteel unit with a PAR lamp inside. A PAR lamp is most commonly described as a 120-volt headlight. In fact, automobile headlights are PARs. PAR stands for Parabolic Aluminized Reflector, and basically it means that it is a self-contained unit with a lamp, lens, and reflector built together. They have worked their way into the stage lighting vocabulary from the rock and roll concert business. They are cheap and comparatively easy to use. A PAR has an elliptical beam of uneven light that a technician has practically no control over since there is nothing that can be done to them to accurately shape the beam or modify the spread of light. They appeal to those technicians and designers who learned their craft doing rock and roll.

Dimmers

The dimming system controls the light intensity of each lighting instrument. Over the last twenty years there have been enormous advances in dimming technology. Computerization has almost completely taken over the lighting field. Due to the incredible miniaturization of current dimming systems, more and more companies are opting to travel with their own dimmers and computer controllers rather than risk the potential grief of house systems. Today's electronic dimming systems do one hundred times more than their manual five-scene preset counterparts of thirty years ago and cost less.

- **Manual dimmers**: Manual dimmers are either resistance or auto-transformer types. They are both operated the same way, although the auto-transformer is a more modern piece of equipment. Both are cumbersome, require several operators, and cannot follow complex, sophisticated cues. When working on a manual board, a lighting designer who is used to working on an electronic dimmer will have to greatly simplify his cues and, therefore, his effectiveness. The only benefit of manual dimmer boards is that they are nearly indestructible.

- **Electronic dimmers:** Electronic dimmers are usually of the SCR (silicon-controlled rectifier) type. The main advantage of the electronic dimmer over a manual dimmer is that it can be remotely controlled by a single operator. Recent advances in technology have reduced the size and cost of dimmers drastically. Electronic dimmers are operated by a remotely-placed controller commonly referred to as a **light board**.

- **Preset controller**: Between the ancient manual dimmer and today's computerized controllers lies the preset controller. In the 1960's and 1970's this was the state of the art in stage dimming. A preset controller has ranks of potentiometers (or pots) with one pot controlling each dimmer. Each rank of pots is called a preset. There may be as few as two presets or as many as ten. One operator was able to set dimmer levels on the presets in advance of another operator moving the controller from cue to cue.

- **Computer controller**: The controller is the element of the system that has undergone the most change. The modern computer-driven controller or light board addresses light levels in increments of 1/100ths instead of 1/10ths. It enables the designer to manipulate entire cues in dozens of ways. It can perform multiple cues simultaneously. It can run cues by itself in times ranging from a fraction of a second to hours in duration. It can record these cues and play them back countless times. The computer controller does all this with precise accuracy each time. In the dark ages of manual control, or even preset control, operator error was a fact of life.

Computer Controller
Strand Lighting

Patch Panels and Circuitry

The maze of cables and connector strips that connect the instruments to the dimmers is known as the circuitry. These cables, either visible or concealed in a raceway, go from the mounting positions on the stage and front of house to the dimmer racks. When working with older technology, there is an intermediate element between the on-stage circuit and the dimmer called the patch panel or Quick-Connect. It is a large panel that often looks like a telephone switchboard. It is a matrix of connections that enables the technician to plug any circuit and thus any instrument into any dimmer. The patch panel is still a common element of many older theatres since they were simply not removed when other elements of the dimming system were upgraded.

■ **Electronic patching**: One of the most important adjuncts to the computerization of stage dimming is the advent of electronic patching (commonly called soft patching). The circuit is directly wired to the dimmer, thus eliminating the patch panel, which is a very expensive piece of equipment. The dimmers are then arranged into usable group or patterns by the use of the dimmer controller which assigns the dimmers electronically into control channels. This may sound complex, but in reality is much simpler than the old patch panel method and avoids the potential of overloaded dimmers since there is an automatic connection between the circuit and the dimmer. The term channel has replaced the term dimmer when describing a dimmable group of instruments.

■ **Cable and connectors**: The spookiest part of presenting a traveling company in your theatre is the integration of their equipment with yours. Only the largest of companies carries all of its own equipment. Everyone else will utilize some combination of their equipment and the theatres' equipment. The point where these two different groups of equipment come together is usually at the connector between the lighting instruments and the dimmable circuits.

There are many different types of connectors used on the stage. There are some types designed specifically for theatres, called grounded pin connectors. These are the preferred type of connector. There are types of specialty connectors adapted for stage use called twist-lock connectors that come in many different configurations of blades and sizes depending on age and amperage. These have the benefit of being able to lock themselves to one another. Some theatres use household connectors called parallel blade or Edison connectors, but they are not recommended for stage use and should be avoided.

The dilemma is that none of these connectors is compatible with the others. To connect a company's instrument to the theatre's cable, or vice versa, it is necessary to make adapters from one connector to another. Most companies that travel with some of their own equipment also travel with adapters to other types of connectors. If your theatre has a particularly strange type of connector, it is critical to let touring companies know of this.

Cable requirements can also become a problem when a touring company mounts a large number of lamps in a position where there are not permanent circuits directly at hand. The most common example of this is for lighting dance, where the bulk of the lighting comes from booms mounted in the wings for sidelighting. Each of these lamps (anywhere from 20 to 100) needs to be cabled to existing house circuits. This can be much more cable than a theatre owns, so everyone needs to be aware of the potential problems.

Appendices

A. SAMPLE TECHNICAL RIDER

Contract Rider

Contract rider between_____ ("Company")
and_____ ("Presenter") Date:_____

Company's staff includes a technical director and stage manager. "Presenter" agrees to cooperate with the Company's stage manager in the preparation and presentation of the performance. In the event of a dispute between the Company stage manager and the "Presenter's" agent or representative having like capacity, the decision of the Company stage manager shall be final. It is nevertheless expressly understood and agreed that the Company stage manager shall not make a demand in excess of the potential of the "Presenter" in relationship to the facility and equipment.

I. *Facility*

A. The performing area must be an area minimum ___x ____.

B. The performing area must have a stage that is deemed safe and acceptable to Company in its sole judgment. It must be smooth, free of splinters, tacks, nails, etc., and not be heavily varnished or waxed. It shall be swept and damp mopped immediately prior to all rehearsals and performances.

C. The stage shall be available to Company __ hours and not used by any other attraction, event, etc., once Company has begun set up until after the final performance and the removal of all Company property and equipment.

D. A quick change area ___ x ___ on both sides of the stage is also required.

II. *Equipment Requirements*

A. Stage equipment, including lighting and sound system as may be in the possession of the theater, shall be readily available for use by Company.

B. Prior to the stage manager's arrival, the presenter shall provide a scaled floor plan of the stage, and if available, a circuit diagram and a diagram of the dimming system showing operational features and capacity of each dimmer. A complete and accurate fly or hanger schedule must be included with the scaled floor plan and all information required in the attached Technical Questionnaire. The Technical Questionnaire shall be returned within ten days of receipt.

C. A "Hanging Plot" shall be sent in advance of the arrival of the Company stage manager and/or lighting designer. Lights must be hung, circuited, and patched prior to the arrival of the Company stage manager and/or lighting designer. The Company stage manager or light designer will supervise all angling and focusing of equipment. If there are any difficulties in meeting the above need, the Company must be informed in advance.

D. The lighting equipment must not be moved or reangled after it has once been set for the Performance(s).

E. Electrical - except as otherwise noted, "Presenter" shall provide:
1. 24 working dimmers *(2.4K capacity each)*.
2. 45-6" x 16" *(plano-convex lens)* ellipsoidal spotlights *(750W)* .
3. 12-6" Fresnels *(500W)*.
4. 2-8" Fresnels *(100W)*.
5. 3-6" x 16" ellipsoidal spotlights with iris *(750W)*.
7. Accompanying color filter frames for all instruments.
8. 8-8 foot light booms with bases.
9. 30-slide hanging side-arms.
10. 1500 feet of #12 or #14 cable sufficient for hanging the light plot.
11. 10 multiple connectors *(i.e., twofers or 3-ways)* .
12. Ladders *(one 'A' frame ladder or cherry picker tall enough to focus lamps at a trim height of __feet)* .
13. At least one follow spot with gels.
14. A slide projector capable of projecting 35mm. slides to stage-screen from rear of house.

Note: Company carries its own gels.

F. Sound - except as otherwise noted, "Presenter" shall provide:
1. Intercom with five sets of headphones *(two-way communication)* located:
   a) center of house, b) stage manager's desk, c) lighting console,
   d) sound booth, e) follow spot booth.
2. Biscuit or small speaker to flyrail.
3. Paging system to all dressing rooms.
4. Amplification with sufficient wattage to drive house system speakers *(minimum-two)* and backstage monitor *(minimum-one)*.
5. 5-standing microphones *(will be set stage right)*.
6. Cable and outlets available with appropriate equipment so each microphone can be independently controlled.
7. A stereo 1/2 track tape recorder for 7-1/2"/ sec. tape.

G. Draperies and masking - except as otherwise noted, "Presenter" shall provide:
1. Act curtain.
2. Four pair legs and borders--black in color.
3. Mid-stage traveler *(set 10' to 15' behind act curtain--dark color)*.
4. Cyclorama or sky drop.

III. Dressing Room Requirements

A. As required by Actors' Equity Association (AEA) *in their safe and sanitary code*: The Company will need adequate space for 6 women and 10 men *(preferably three dressing rooms.)* Dressing rooms should have hot and cold running water, tables, chairs, mirrors, adequate light for applying stage makeup, and clothes racks for the costumes. Dressing rooms must be clean, sanitary, and absolutely private; must be reserved for the exclusive use of the Company during their stay; and must have direct access to the stage out of public view. The restrooms provided for the actors must be separate facilities from those provided for the audiences and should contain adequate paper supplies and soap. *All dressing rooms must be cleaned and dusted prior to the arrival of the Company.*

IV. Personnel Requirements - except as otherwise noted, "Presenter" shall provide minimum requirements for technical assistance for the Company:

A. Head Electrician

B. Assistant Electrician *(if required for operation of performance)*

C. Flyman

D. Soundman

E. Followspot operator

F. Prop man

G. Any additional personnel as required by the house

H. Wardrobe personnel

V. Miscellaneous

A. Two 6' x 3' tables shall be provided at stage right for props.

B. Adequate security must be provided to insure safety of costumes and props.

C. House staff must clear with Company's stage manager or general manager before opening the house. Company will open the house at least 30 minutes before show time.

D. All visitors shall be excluded from the theater during set-up and rehearsal periods unless written permission is obtained from Company in advance.

E. Adequate fresh drinking water within a comfortable distance of the stage shall be provided.

F. Parking space for one bus and three other vehicles must be reserved for Company as near the performing area as possible.

Agreed By Presenter _____

B. SAMPLE TECHNICAL QUESTIONNAIRE

[Note: Due to space considerations, this form has been condensed and not all spaces for responses have been included.]

Presenter Contacts

Name of performance space _____

Address _____

City_____State_____Zip Code _____

Name of institution, college, or organization _____

Please describe how to locate the performance space *(address, campus location,*

etc.) ; include map if needed _____

_____

Person responsible for this engagement:

Name _____Position _____

Office Telephone_____Home _____

Person to whom the light plot should be sent:

Name _____Position _____

Office Telephone _____Home _____

Address _____

Person completing this questionnaire:

Name _____Position _____

Office Telephone_____Home _____

I. General Information

A. Auditorium capacity: Main floor ___ + Balcony ___ = Total _____

B. Load-in point: ( ) Directly on stage ( ) Scene shop ( ) Other. Describe _____

C. Is loading area: ( ) Above stage level *(dock height)* ( ) Stage level
      ( ) Other. Describe _____

D. Comments on load-in problems *(stairs, narrow door, etc.)* : _____

E. Number semi-trailer trucks accommodated in your dock at one time: _____

F. Is a union crew required? _____

II. Dressing Rooms

A. Total number of dressing rooms:

Type	How many?	Dimensions	Can accommodate
Principal	_____	_____	_____
Soloist	_____	_____	_____
Chorus	_____	_____	_____

B. Where are the dressing rooms? *(Note: Dressing rooms for six men and eleven women are required)*
      ( ) Stage level ( ) Above stage level ( ) Below stage level.
      Describe distance and path from stage to dressing rooms: _____

C. Are there page monitors in each room? _____

D. Are the rooms equipped with? ( ) Mirrors ( ) Make up lights ( ) Sinks
    ( ) Showers ( ) Wardrobe racks ( ) Adequate heat

E. Can quick-change booths be set-up backstage with lights and mirrors? _____

III. Stage Dimensions

A. Proscenium opening: Width_____   Height_____

B. Stage:
    1. Depth from plaster line *(upstage edge of proscenium wall)* to back wall: ____
    2. Depth from front apron to plaster line: _____
    3. Wing space right: _____
    4. Wing space left: _____
    5. Height from stage floor to grid *(or ceiling if dead hung)* : _____
    6. Usual trim height *(floor to bottom of borders or teasers)* : _____
    7. List all usable entrances to the stage *(with dimensions)* : _____
    8. Comments on stage space *(columns, permanent set storage, permanent
        piano storage, permanent stage managers' booths, etc.)* : _____

A. Do you have a fly system? ( ) Yes ( ) No

B. If you have a fly system:
    1. What type is it? ( ) counterweight ( ) hemp ( ) electrical winch
    2. Is it ( ) single purchase ( ) double purchase?
    3. Weight capacity each arbor? _____
    4. How many lines sets *(battens)* are available in the total system: _____
    5. Describe lines that are unavailable due to permanent storage: _____
    6. How high will lines fly? _____
    7. How close to the floor will the pipes come in? _____
    Please include a hanger log of the stage if at all possible. This is very important!

C. Act curtain *(house curtain)* :
    1. Does it ( ) fly ( ) draw?
    2. Is it ( ) manual ( ) motorized? If motorized, what is the cycle name? _____
    3. What is its color and material? _____
    4. Additional comments: _____

V. Masking (curtains)

A. Legs *(side, vertical masking drapes)*
    1. How many pair of legs are necessary to mask the stage? _____
    2. How many pair of legs do you have available? _____
    3. What are their hanging dimensions? _____x _____
    4. What color and material are they? _____
    5. What condition are they? _____
    6. Are the legs permanently hung? _____
    7. If the legs are permanently hung, or if there is an unusual leg hang, list it
        below: *(distance from plaster line)*
        a. Set #1_____   d. Set #4 _____
        b. Set #2_____   e. Set #5 _____
        c. Set #3_____

B. Borders or teasers *(overhead, horizontal masking drapes)*
1. How many borders are necessary to mask the stage? _____
2. How many borders do you have available? _____
3. What are their hanging dimensions? _____
4. What color and material are they? _____
5. What is their condition? _____
6. Are they permanently hung? _____
7. If they are permanently hung, or if there is an unusual border hang, list it
   below: *(distance from plaster line)*
   a. #1. _____   d. #4 _____
   b. #2. _____   e. #5 _____
   c. #3. _____

C. Backings
1. Do you have a curved cyclorama? ( ) yes ( ) no
   a. What are its dimensions? _____
   b. What color and material is it? _____
   c. What is its condition? _____
   d. What is its distance from the plaster line? _____
   e. Is there a cross-over behind the cyclorama? _____
   f. Can the cyclorama be moved or struck? _____

[Usage note: Repeat above section for flat sky-drop as applicable.]

D. Additional comments: _____

VI. Lighting Systems

A. Dimmers
1. Brand name of dimmers: _____
2. Type: ( ) solid state *(SCR or Triac)* ( ) auto-transformer
   ( ) resistance
3. Total number of dimmers: _____
4. List dimmers by wattage capacity:
   _____ dimmers at _____ watts capacity each
   _____ dimmers at _____ watts capacity each
   _____ dimmers at _____ watts capacity each
5. How old is the system? _____ years
6. In what condition are the dimmers? *(How reliable are they?)* _____

B. Control board
1. Is it ( ) memory ( ) preset ( ) manual?
2. List brand name: _____
3. List model name if known: _____
4. If it is a memory board:
   a. Is it programmed by ( ) a keyboard ( ) potentiometers ( ) both?
   b. Does it have sub-masters? _____ If so, how many? _____
   c. Does it have assignable control channels? _____ If so, how many? _____
   d. Does it have soft patch capabilities? _____
   e. Describe back-up system, if applicable: _____
   f. List any unusual features: _____
   g. How reliable is it? _____
5. If it is a preset board:

a. List the number of presets _____

b. Describe the kind of presets *(cards, pots, wheels, etc.)* _____

c. Is there a grand master controller? _____

d. Are there sub-masters? _____ If so, how many? _____

e. Is the fade controller ( ) cross fade ( ) split fade ( ) pile on ( ) time?

6. What is the location of the control board? _____

7. Is there a remote control station? _____

C. Patch panel

1. How do you patch circuits to dimmers? ( ) dimmer per circuit ( ) pin and plug,
   ( ) patch panel ( ) quick connect ( ) hard wired

2. Brand name of patch panel _____

3. Where is it located? _____

4. Total number of circuits in system _____

5. Is there a F.O.H. disconnect in the patch panel? _____

D. Power source

1. Is there a Company switch for tying-in road boards? _____

2. If there is a Company switch:

   a. Is it three-phase or single-phase? _____

   b. What is the amperage per leg? _____

   c. Where is it located in relation to the stage? _____

3. If there is no Company switch:

   a. Where is the closest source of electricity to the stage: minimum ( ) 400
      amps. 120 VAC of three phase per leg OR ( ) 250 amps. 120 VAC of
      three phase per leg _____

   b. Describe source *(power panel, transformer, existing dimmer buss bars,
      etc.)* _____

   c. Do you require your electrician to tie into this power source? _____

VII. LIGHTING EQUIPMENT

A. Lighting instruments

Quantity	Type	Lens Diam. X	Focal Length	Single or Double Lens	Wattage	Brand
	Leko*	6" X				
	Leko*	6" X				
	Leko*	8" X				
	Leko*	X				
	Leko*	X				
	Fresnel	6"		####		
	Fresnel	8"		####		
	Fresnel			####		
	Scoop**	####		####		
	Beam Projector	####		####		

*Ellipsoidal Reflector Spotlight   **Ellipsoidal Reflector Floodlight

B. Strip lights: Do you have strip lights? ( ) yes ( ) no
    1. How many sections? _____
    2. Length of each section: _____
    3. Number of circuits in each section: _____
    4. Wattage of each lamp: _____
    5. Are strips permanently hung? _____
    6. If permanently hung, list distances from plaster line _____

C. Connectors
    1. What type of connectors are used in your lighting system?
       a. Pin connector: ( ) 2-pin *(ungrounded)* ( ) 3-pin *(grounded)*
          ( ) 3-pin locking *(Hargelock)*
       b.Twist lock: ( ) 2-prong *(ungrounded)* ( ) 15A ( ) 20A ( ) 30A
          ( ) 3-prong *(ground OUT)* ( ) 15A ( ) 20A ( ) 30A
          ( ) 3-prong *(ground IN)* ( ) 15A ( ) 20A ( ) 30A
       c. Parallel blade *(household or edison)* : ( ) 2-prong *(ungrounded)*
          ( ) 3-prong *(grounded)* ( ) stage plug *(slip plug)* ( ) 20A ( ) 30A
          ( ) other *(describe and diagram)* _____

If you have twistlock connectors, please diagram the configuration of the blades and grounding tabs.

VIII. Lighting Positions

A. Onstage lighting positions
    1. First electric or bridge
       a. Distance from plaster line _____
       b. Number of *different* circuits _____
       c. Does it fly?____ If no, list height _____
       d. List any permanently mounted instruments: _____
[Usage note: Repeat above section for second, third, fourth electrics as applicable.]
    5. Cyclorama lighting
       a. From what pipe do you light the cyclorama? _____
       b. Distance from this pipe to cyclorama _____
       c. Do you have a cyc pit or trough? _____
       d. If yes, list distance from plaster line _____
       e. What kind of instrument do you light the cyc with? _____
       Type of instrument _____
       Number of Instruments _____
       Wattage of each lamp _____
       Number of units required to get an even wash _____
    6. Tormentor or cove position
       a. Distance from plaster line _____
       b. Distance off-stage from center line _____
       c. Height range from floor_____to _____
    7. Side booms or ladders
       a. How many do you have? _____
       b. Describe their locations _____
       c. How many *different* circuits does each have? _____

8. Floor pockets
  a. How many do you have? _____
  b. What type of connectors? _____
  c. Number of separate circuits in each floor pocket_____
  d. Are they ganged side to side? _____
  e. Are these pockets the source of circuits used for side lighting? _____
  f. Describe the location of all floor pockets _____

B. Front of house lighting positions
  1. Beam slot #1 *(ceiling slots or ports)*
    a. Distance from plaster line _____
    b. Height above stage level _____
    c. Number of *different* circuits _____
    d. Describe all permanently mounted instruments _____

[Usage note: Repeat above section for beam slots #2 and 3, balcony front (balcony rail) as applicable.]

  5. House booms *(vertical pipes or ladders in the house)*
    a. Describe their positions in relation to the stage _____
    b. Height above stage level _____
    c. Number of *different* circuits _____
    d. Describe all permanently mounted instruments _____

IX. Sound System
A. Do you use your sound system for the reproduction of music recordings? _____
  1. How would you objectively rate the sound created by your system? _____
  2. How reliable is your sound system? _____

B. Amplifiers
  1. Brand name_____Model _____
  2. What is its *(their)* age? _____
  3. What is its *(their)* condition? _____
  4. Is the system stereo? _____
  5. What is its rated wattage per channel? _____

C. Pre-amplifiers *(mixers)*
  1. Brand name _____
  2. What is its *(their)* age? _____
  3. What is its *(their)* condition? _____
  4. How many channels are available? _____
  5. Are bass and treble adjustable? _____
  6. Where is control board located? _____

D. Speakers
  1. Brand name _____
  2. What is its *(their)* age? _____
  3. What is its *(their)* condition? _____
  4. How many channels are available? _____
  5. Are bass and treble adjustable? _____
  6. Where is control board located? _____

E. Reel-to-reel tape deck
    1. Brand name_____ Model _____
    2. What is its age? _____
    3. What is its condition? _____
    4. Is it stereo? _____
    5. Number of tracks ( ) one ( ) two ( ) four ( ) eight
    6. What speed does it run? ( ) 3-3/4 ( ) 7-1/2 ( ) 15 ips

F. Other equipment
    1. Describe any other types of additional sound equipment available *(dolby, DBX, equalizers etc.)* _____

G. Communications
    1. Do you have a communication system? _____
    2. How does it operate? *(head-sets, biscuits, phone handsets)* _____
    3. Brand name _____Model _____
    4. What is its age? _____
    5. What is its condition? _____
    6. How many stations are there? _____
    7. Where are they located? _____

X. Miscellaneous Items

A. Stage Floor
    1. Is the floor resilient? _____
    2. Describe floor surface *(material & condition)* _____
    3. Describe the floor support structure *(if known)* _____
    4. Are there traps or elevators in the floor? _____
    5. Do you have access to a portable dance floor? _____
    6. If so, brand name? _____condition?_____color? _____
    7. Notes _____

B. Do you have a ladder, cherry picker, or rolling scaffold high enough to reach the on-stage electric when they are at their trim height *(approximately 28')?* ___

C. Please make any other comments about your performance space which will be helpful to us.

Single purchase counterweight system

1. Headblock for lift line and hand line
2. Loftblocks
3. Wire rope lift lines
4. Batten
5. Endless line/hand line
6. Counterweight arbor
7. Locking rail
8. Floorblock/tension block
9. Tee-track guides
10. Loading platform

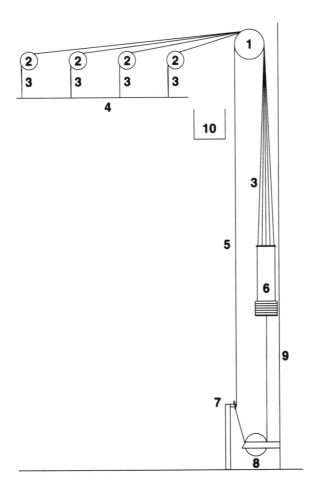

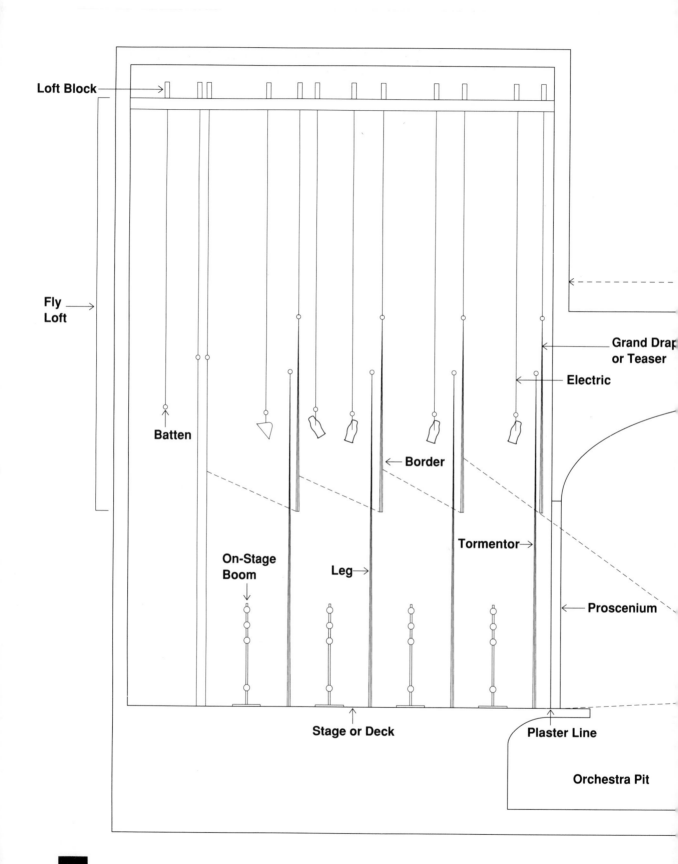

Loft Block

Fly Loft

Batten

On-Stage Boom

Leg

Border

Grand Drap or Teaser

Electric

Tormentor

Proscenium

Stage or Deck

Plaster Line

Orchestra Pit

*A side view of the stage
as seen through the
center of the stage.
Used to determine the
proper placement of
scenic elements and
lighting instruments.*

Front of House (F.O.H)

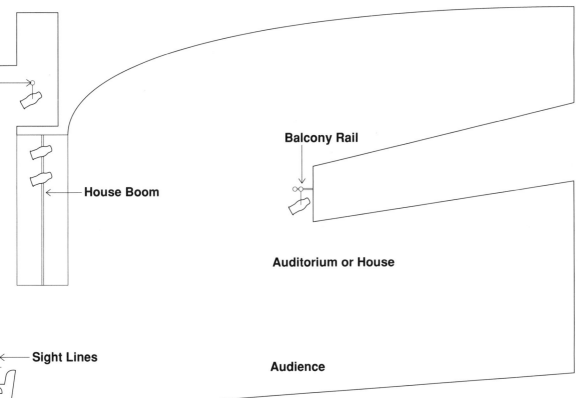

Balcony Rail

House Boom

Auditorium or House

Sight Lines

Audience

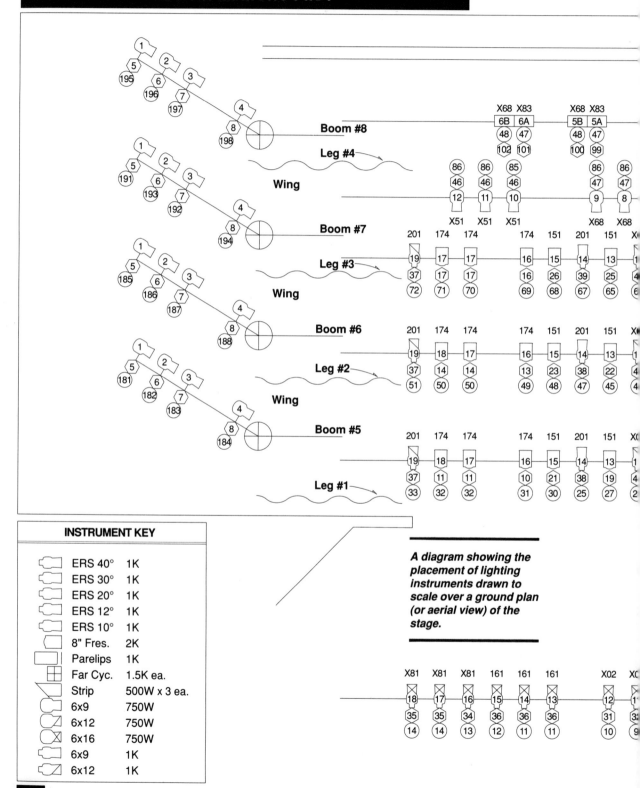

A diagram showing the placement of lighting instruments drawn to scale over a ground plan (or aerial view) of the stage.

INSTRUMENT KEY

	ERS 40°	1K
	ERS 30°	1K
	ERS 20°	1K
	ERS 12°	1K
	ERS 10°	1K
	8" Fres.	2K
	Parelips	1K
	Far Cyc.	1.5K ea.
	Strip	500W x 3 ea.
	6x9	750W
	6x12	750W
	6x16	750W
	6x9	1K
	6x12	1K

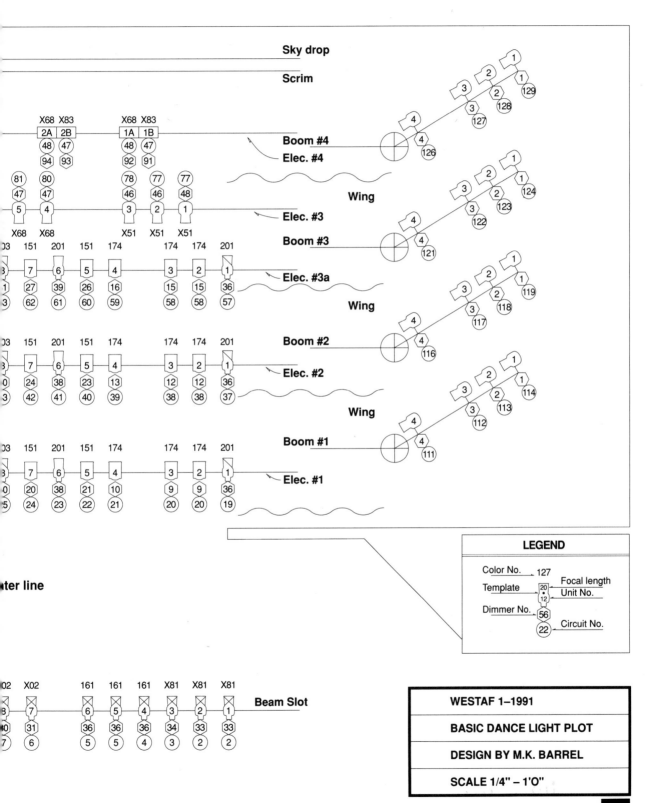

Sky drop

Scrim

Boom #4
Elec. #4

Wing

Elec. #3
Boom #3

Elec. #3a

Wing

Boom #2
Elec. #2

Wing

Boom #1
Elec. #1

ter line

Beam Slot

LEGEND

Color No. — 127
Template — 20 ← Focal length
• ← Unit No.
12
Dimmer No. — 56
22 — Circuit No.

WESTAF 1–1991
BASIC DANCE LIGHT PLOT
DESIGN BY M.K. BARREL
SCALE 1/4" – 1'O"

F. HANGER LOG

The base hanger log is generated by the presenter to give detailed information on the rigging system to the company. The company takes the base hanger log, modifies it according to their requirements, and returns it to the presenter. This completed hanger log is used to prepare the theatre for the performances. Shaded lines on the completed hanger log indicate additions or changes from the base hanger log.

Base Hanger Log

Proscenium 28'9"x57'6"   *Denotes Standard Hang   Typical Auditorium
Grid: 62'3"   Pipes Typical 62'   State College

Distance Plaster Line	Line #	Description of Goods	Center Line	Trim Height	Piece Size	Weight Approx.
0'9"	0	*Act Curtain (Guillotine)			30x68	1200
1'4"	1	*Grand Drape (House Border)		22'-26'	12x70	900
1'11"	2	*Leg #1 Black (Torm)	22'	Deck	32x12	200
2'6"	3					
3'10"	4	*#1 Electric (Flys only to 55')				600
5'1"	5					
5'8"	6					
6'3"	7	*Front Screen (Roll-Up)				
6'10"	8					
7'5"	9	*Traveler (Track) Black Velour	C/L	Deck	32x65	900
8'0"	10					

Typical Completed Hanger Log

Proscenium 28'9"x57'6"   *Denotes Standard Hang   The Dream/Ophelia
Grid: 62'3"   Pipes Typical 62'   Typical Auditorium State College

Distance Plaster Line	Line #	Description of Goods	Center Line	Trim Height	Piece Size	Weight Approx.
0'9"	0	*Act Curtain (Guillotine)			30x68	1200
1'4"	1	*Grand Drape (House Border)		24	12x70	900
1'11"	2	*Leg #1 Black (Torm)	22'	Deck	32x12	200
2'6"	3					
3'10"	4	*#1 Road Electric		TBA		700
5'1"	5	#1 Cross-Over Cable		38'		180
5'8"	6					
6'3"	7	#1 Dream Border (Over Projection Screen)		TBA	12x65	100
6'10"	8					
7'5"	9	#2 Black Leg (House)	21'	Deck	32x12	200
8'0"	10	#1 Dream Leg	21'	Deck	33x14	100